For Peter Carolin whose support enabled these artefacts to be built and who helped so many others during his term as Professor of Architecture at the University of Cambridge.

ON CERTAIN POSSIBILITIES FOR THE IRRATIONAL EMBELLISHMENT OF A TOWN
TEN URBAN ARTEFACTS

introduction **Peter Carl**	4
artefact 1 **Vendor's Box** – Peter Ferretto	10
artefact 2 **Writing Booth** – Tom Emerson	20
artefact 3 **Spring** – Nicholas Zervoglos	28
artefact 4 **Pavement Lights** – Ben Adams	38
artefact 5 **Borderline** – David Grandorge	44
artefact 6 **Day Bed** – Emma Huckett	54
artefact 7 **Leaner** – José Esteves de Matos	64
artefact 8 **Bitsop** – Joseph Marinescu	74
artefact 9 **Camera Obscura Desk** – Anat Talmor	80
artefact 10 **Crystal Bench** – Erica Cotton	88

ON
CERTAIN
POSSIBILITIES
FOR
THE
IRRATIONAL
EMBELLISHMENT
OF
A
TOWN
TEN
URBAN
ARTEFACTS

THE CASUAL READER WILL BE TEMPTED
PRESENTED HERE WITHIN THE WELL-ESTA
LIFE-STYLE. HOWEVER, THESE WORKS AR
TASTE. THEY ARE VEHICLES OF EXPLORAT
INTO THE BACKGROUND OF PUBLIC SITU
ARE WELL-RECOUNTED BY ERIC PARRY, I
DUCTION STRIVES TO UNDERSTAND HOW
THE LARGER CULTURAL INTERESTS.

INCLUDE THE REMARKABLE ARTEFACTS
SHED PROTOCOLS OF ART / COMMERCE /
OT THE RESULTS OF A PROCESS AIMED AT
OR RESEARCH, METAPHORICAL PORTALS
ONS. THEIR INDIVIDUAL THEMATIC FIELDS
S TEXT FOR EACH PROJECT. THIS INTRO-
E CARE REGARDING MAKING RELATES TO

Making

Paradoxically, the modernist attunement to austerity in its artefacts both emphasises constructional issues (as 'tectonics') and obscures them (within cowlings or by hiding the joints and fixings, often in fact making construction quite difficult). This is usually for the sake of either maintenance or a cultural idea. Exemplifying the latter category, early modernist chairs present a spectrum of mentalities which moves from discipline (Mies) to restraint (Jacobsen) to abstract space (Rietveld). The sequence also traces a descending quotient of erotic content. If all have a 'primitivist' ancestor in something like the chair of Van Gogh, the self-assigned obligation to find a new equivalent allowed a promiscuous mingling of the vita *povera* of the Shakers with late medieval Japan, and both of these with engineering. The Miesian chair demands isolation from stone planes; Scandinavian furniture accommodates the mess of everyday life; the Rietveld strives for invisibility in an orthogonal continuum of primary colours. Constructionally, the Miesian chair is silent, elegant and neurotic: its discrete welds, tensioned metal tubes and stretched hide are ever wary of a person fat or gregarious. Scandinavian chairs are reliable, friendly, wooden things, fond of smoothness. The Rietveld chair would prefer to be held together by concepts alone, resolutely dispensing with both gravity and materials.

If, then, it might be Mies in the salon (or board-room), Jacobsen in the dining-room (or at the desk), and as an objet-d'art, we recognise also a spectrum of bourgeois proclivities: portentous authority, earnest utility and faintly ecstatic aesthetic contemplation. The promised cultural revolution which might be achieved by sitting in these chairs was best understood by Jacques Tati. The revolution's morning hang-over was the Pop and plastic of the post-war period, whose irony and kitsch were dimmed by the melancholia of the material's ubiquity and inevitably eager colours. Plastic had its highest calling in equipment. From military (or Bond) matte black to inoffensive-to-any-decor beige, plastic has now come full circle to the sci-fi chrysalis yoghurt-flavoured iMac, whose translucent shroud protects exotic components devoted to relentless consumption of numbers: a large light-bulb engorged with termites.

The only discourse regarding the implements, furniture and panelling of contemporary life which is able to avoid the derive into unstable allusions and the banalities of desire is that devoted to making. Here the conversation is dominated by sobriety, attentiveness, purpose, precision, material properties, quantitative exactitude, cause-and-effect, structural integrity, economy, substantial results and fine judgements based on craft experience and/or technical know-how. Seeming to be everything the rest of the culture is not, this discourse – mostly as technology– has served as the measure of every cultural relativism since Manetti's valorisation of homo faber in the fifteenth century. Since the Encyclopedie of Diderot and D'Alembert, there has prevailed a tendency to measure history according to technological innovation, even to thinking of culture and history as capable of being 'made.'

This delusion depends upon the belief that culture could be transformed into nature-as-universal-resource, including people. The terms 'labour' and 'the people' gained prominence together when making became mass repetitive behaviour (as opposed to the cultural typicalities of the traditional crafts) and when it became clear that the workers did not comprise the massed choirs of a drama of social redemption enacted in the naves of factories. Yet there is a culture of making within its own theatre of operations (roughly the list above). More importantly, there is a manifold of subtle ways in which the fine judgements of making-well are more than a matter of material resources, tools and available skills. Like judgements in morals or politics they are themselves culturally conditioned.

This is the domain of making explored in the projects of this book. For example, there is potential wit in a joint excessively precise or in deciding whether a material 'wants to be' crude or refined, slightly weak or implacably strong, remote or solicitous of attention. Such judgements do not transpire within an introverted speculation but rather as a dialogue with the situations in which the artefacts participate. Unlike the early modernist furniture, the meaning is not intrinsic to the qualities and configuration of the artefact itself; but rather it is extrinsic, astutely entering into the multiple 'claims' of the materials, the exigencies of construction, the situations. The movement from a pile of materials to human situations is necessarily a metaphoric process. The designer's 'freedom' is a freedom – for attentiveness to others, not unlike one's role in a conversation, or as a host.

Artefacts for Public Situations

The decay of public life has been marked by the 'fall' of public man and by decanting the fundamentally political character of the public realm into the social (Sennet, Arendt). It is played out in the 'non-places' of concourses and malls which deploy architecture as the mute support for signs and simulacra (Auge and Baudrillard). Metropolitan public spaces are seen to be flowing with crowds of people 'without qualities' (Musil), able to find meaning only in privacy and in a form of domesticity conceived to be a refuge from the alienation of a public domain finding its essence in traffic. The importance of the domestic and its receptivity to art was a significant aspect of the theatre of the early modernist revolution, for whose mise-en-scene its furniture was a principal element.

It is, therefore, the singular merit of the works presented here to have colonised the gap between the customary theoretical extremes of public and private, much as they discovered a gap in the domain of making between 'technics and aesthetics.' The situational understanding finds most creative what is otherwise a theoretical hiatus. Inspired by Vesely's work in phenomenological hermeneutics, this insight arises from within the concreteness of life as it is found in actual streets and public settings; it is a 'bottom-up' argument which immerses itself in the messiness of praxis, its conflicts and accommodations. It is an insight which runs counter to the proclivity for totalising theoretical generalisations embodied in extravagant imagery and language by which modernism – from Le Corbusier to the recent advocacy of 'flowspace' as a vehicle of freedom – has regularly offered salvation from a life deemed ignoble, disorganised, unhealthy, slow, out-of-date, lacking in coherence or purpose.

Not being concerned with salvation, there is also an accommodation with the transient, the accidental, the noisy, the illegal and, in short, with finitude. At the same time, the works published here avoid the patronising irony of Venturi's 'popular culture' by accepting the creativity of the anonymous among-one-other of praxis, the latent for-one-another of an urban solidarity that may no longer be openly celebrated but nonetheless survives. 'Anonymity' is usually taken to be an attribute of alienation, for which the customary antidote is intimacy, with a terminal end-point in 'the body'; but a situational understanding takes for granted that the conditions of freedom are ever implicated in the claims of involvement, and that involvement ranges from aggression or casual proximity through fellowship and collaboration to intimacy. Finally, this anonymity connotes the typicalities with which the involvements of praxis are saturated. From postures and gestures through conversations, allusions and misunderstandings, the moment of decorum points to an order which even the supposedly 'chaotic' city obeys; it points to what is ultimately common within the play of differences. The plurality of involvements respects the structure of typicalities (or analogies), the continuity which ultimately comes to rest in the anonymity of the world in which we are always already participants.

The role of public artefacts in this communicative order is exemplified quite literally in a small episode from Joyce's *Ulysses*. Crossing Mountjoy Square, Father Conmee remembers a letter to the father provincial. He accosts three boys, exchanges pleasantries, and asks one of them to post the letter in a red pillar-box:

> But mind you don't post yourself into the box little man, he said. The boys six-eyed Father Conmee and laughed... Master Brunny Lynam ran across the road and put Father Conmee's letter to father provincial into the mouth of the bright red letterbox, Father Conmee smiled and nodded and smiled and walked along Mountjoy Square east.

The looking, talking and mailing traverse the distances between the spontaneity of the boys, the awkward religious authority of Conmee and the institutional remoteness of the pillar-box, whose official 'mouth' alludes to those of the father provincial, the Pope, or God, but also to the mouth of any communicant at the altar-rail, where the transubstantiation makes the wafer a little man in the box.

Of course the late Victorian pillar-box actually represented the Crown; but, as a participant in this faintly ceremonial occasion, it incarnates the general institutional principle of benevolent authority and dependable service: divine Grace delivers souls as does the Royal Mail letters. Joyce's humour mocks trust in institutional authority of this kind whilst also fearing the loss of hope in its disappearance: souls, letters and meanings are much more likely to go astray if left to their own devices, cast free from their institutional obligations.

All of the artefacts in this book are situated in the post-institutional order where data, information, knowledge and wisdom seem noisily to insist upon their equivalence. Yet these artefacts offer themselves to the distracted mobility of the public imagination like the pillar-box, as potential openings to the obscured conditions of stability. Grand references such as the transubstantiation are occluded by the ruptured channels of institutional mediation; but, with the Surrealists' instinct for oneiric worlds hidden within laconic reality, the narratives unfolded through these works expose the immediacy of concrete circumstances to deeper forces. Whether it is with rough humour or quiet wit, with elaborate mechanical ceremony or the discretion of a good waiter, with gentle pressure at the shoulder or the mysterious emanation of light or water from metal, all of these projects arise from an openness to the given conditions, from the vulnerability and courage of generosity. In the best sense, they are street-wise.

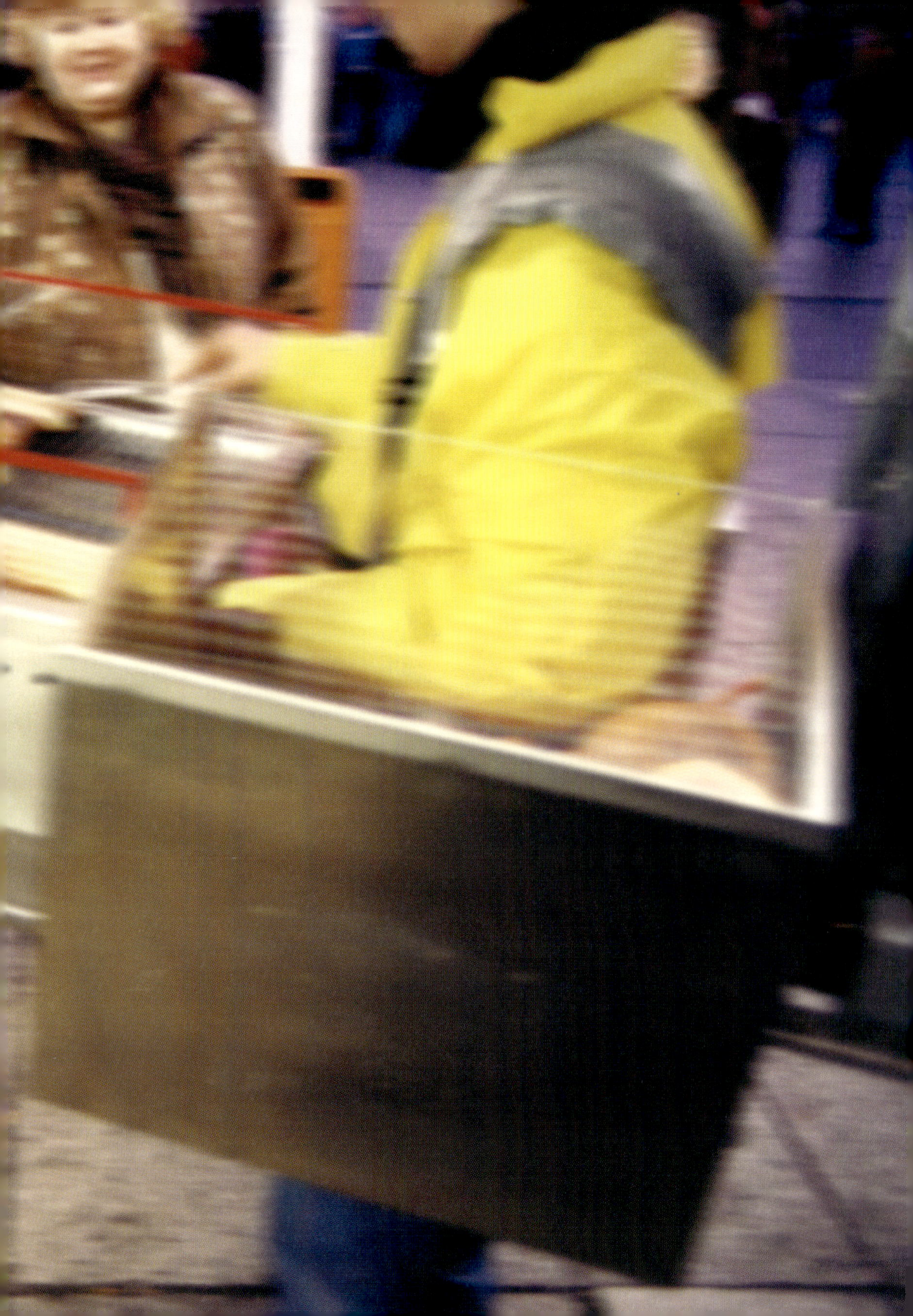

Vendor's Box – Peter Ferretto

Peter had two particular interests that drew him to the design of street furniture. The first was his family links with Como in Northern Italy, and the strong association of that province to furniture design and fabrication. The other interest was in the urban condition which, after studying in the raw, vibrant context of Liverpool, he had furthered whilst working in Paris where he became absorbed by the richness of street life and particularly the cycles of urban change associated with flea markets there. Peter's *Vendor's Box* began as an investigation of these settings.

The market lies at the root of the concept of urbanism. Its footprint is to be found wherever in a dense urban condition a looser spatial arrangement of buildings is evident – at the widening of a road where a junction has developed into a space or between two situational conditions. In the nineteenth and twentieth centuries the incision of transportation systems into the preexisting urban fabric, first through rail and then the aerial highway, has created tracts of semi-inhabitable land. Examples of are ever present – the concrete and steel piloti of overpasses and city highways offering a more porous space than their Victorian brick arched precursors. A beneficial result has been the space made available for street markets.

Importantly, by offering a foothold in the world of commerce and retail to urban migrants where rental or purchase of property would otherwise exclude them and drive up the cost of their produce, a rare opportunity is created for social interchange between those who have and those who do not. One of the most intoxicating urban scene changes is the transformation of a market from full flow to emptiness and vice versa. At one moment the space echoes to the sound of one's own footfall – punctuated by long uninterrupted vistas – the next you are swamped by a hundred actions within a few square metres, the street surface having all but disappeared with the seduction of the shopper in full spate. Peter carefully recorded this transformation in two cities, in Paris at the market of Porte de Clingnancourt and in Berlin at Alexander Platz.

In the first place the analysis revealed the more or less official setting up and clearing away – the erection of the stall frameworks and awnings. This was followed the next morning by the clearing and cleaning of the market using high powered water hoses on this occasion and, perhaps, crowd control on another. In the second was the activity of the market fringe – those without official sanction or space whose trappings and fragile furniture revealed dexterity and invention. Amongst this group Peter discovered the sausage vendor whose ingenious equipment included a gas canister strapped to his back fuelling the cantilevered frying range attached to his waist, allowing his arms and hands the freedom to control cooking, wrapping and exchanging. This mobile kitchen required only the stability of his legs, no road or market tax. The other was the group trading off instantly collapsible surfaces whose custom of predominantly illicit goods and gambling was subject to the harassment of the 'flic' and had, as a result, developed a miraculously rapid disappearance act. The observation of these groups carrying their commercial life in or on a box, having a surface to deal from and being able to move on as rapidly as possible, formed the seeds of the brief for the *Vendor's Box*.

BRIDE MACHINE

1 ▶ **2** ▶ **3** ▶

Alphabetic units

LETTER BOX (ALPHABET) | DRAFT PISTONS | TRIPLE CIPHER | NETS — govern alphabet and terms of the Pendu femelle's commands

BRIDE
ARBOR-TYPE
STEAM ENGINE
SKELETON
PENDU FEMELLE
VIRGIN

gives birth to 2nd blossoming

WASP / SEX CYLINDER — controls atmospheric pressure / secretes love gasoline from dew (by osmosis) / controls spark of desire magneto

CAGE — contains filament material

BLACK

SHOT
PULL

WHERE IS THE BLACK CARD ?

mirror image of splash

MOTOR WITH QUITE FEEBLE CYLINDERS — controls arbor-type

filament material to Handler

RESERVOIR — of love gasoline

DESIRE-MAGNETO — emits artificial sparks

BRIDE'S CLOTHES | HORIZON

GILLED COOLER | ISOLATING PLATES | WILSON-LINCOLN SYSTEM

HANDLER
TRAINER OF GRAVITY
JUGGLER

BOXING MATCH
geared system

RED

SCISSORS — control splash

ARCHITECTONIC BASE FOR THE BRIDE

PARASOLS DRAINAGE SLOPES SIEVES

OCULIST CHARTS
OCULIST WITNESSES

BACHELOR MACHINE

Bachelors transmit commands by electric process

CAPILLARY TUBES
solidify and cut illuminating gas into spangles

WATERFALL

spangles converted into liquid scattered suspension

CEMETERY OF UNIFORMS AND LIVERIES
MALIC MOULDS
EROS' MATRIX — mould illuminating gas

PUMP
CHUTE
WEIGHT WITH HOLES

Priest
Department-store delivery boy
Gendarme
Cuirassier
Policeman
Undertaker
Flunkey
Busboy
Station-master

CHARIOT
SLEIGH
SLIDE
GLIDER
recites litanies
opens scissors

CHAIN WATER WILSON MILL

fall of bottle operates slide

CHOCOLATE MACHINE
CHOCOLATE GRINDER
Bayonet
Necktie
Rollers
Louis XV chassis

PLANES OF FLOW
SPLASH
FALLS
DINS
CRASHES

RED CROSS

BOTTLE — of variable density

RUNNERS

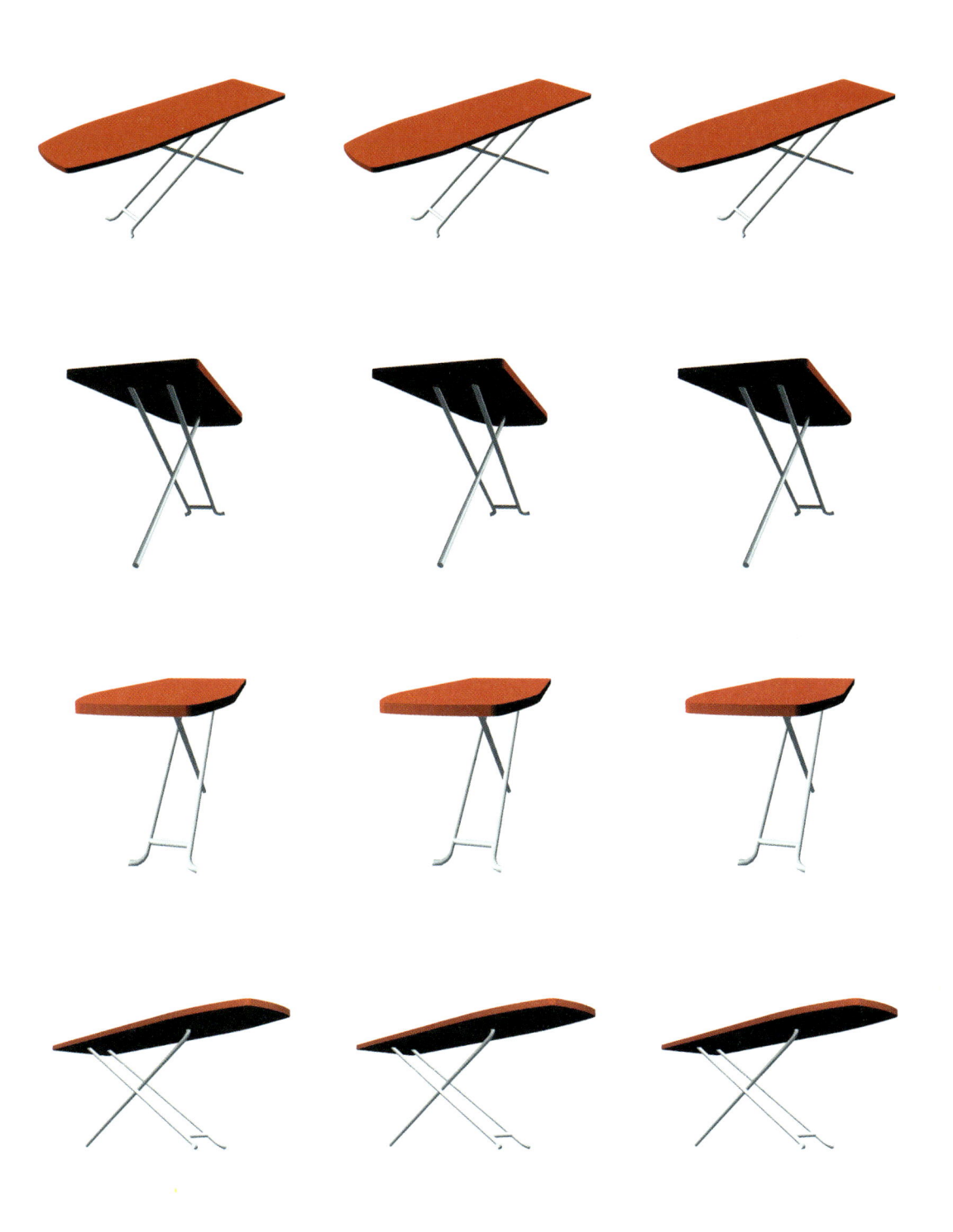

Vendor's Box

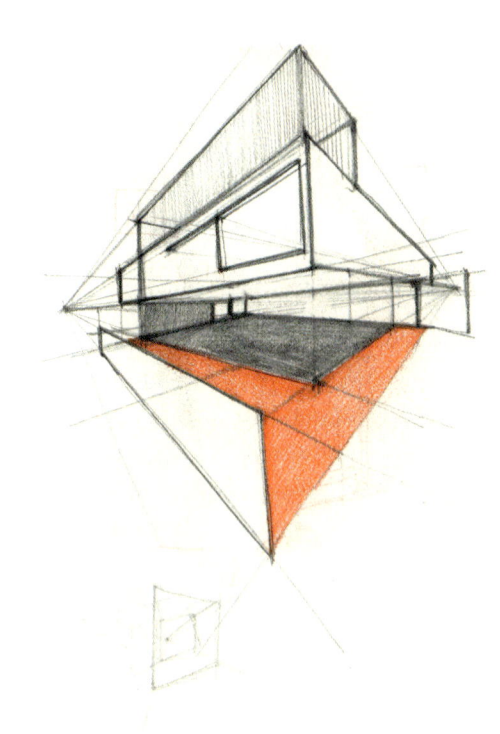

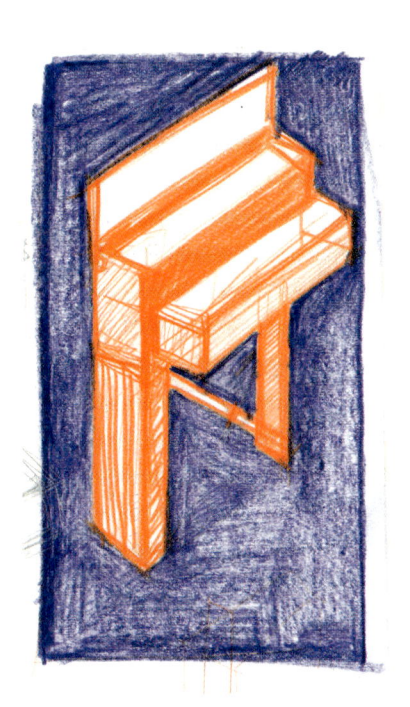

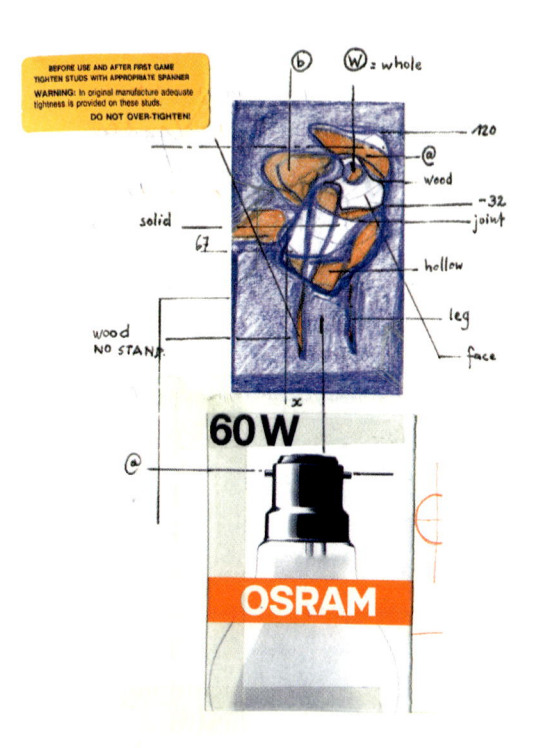

14 On Certain Possibilities for the Irrational Embellishment of a Town Ten Urban Artefacts

to act as a tower. Ruota della fortuna

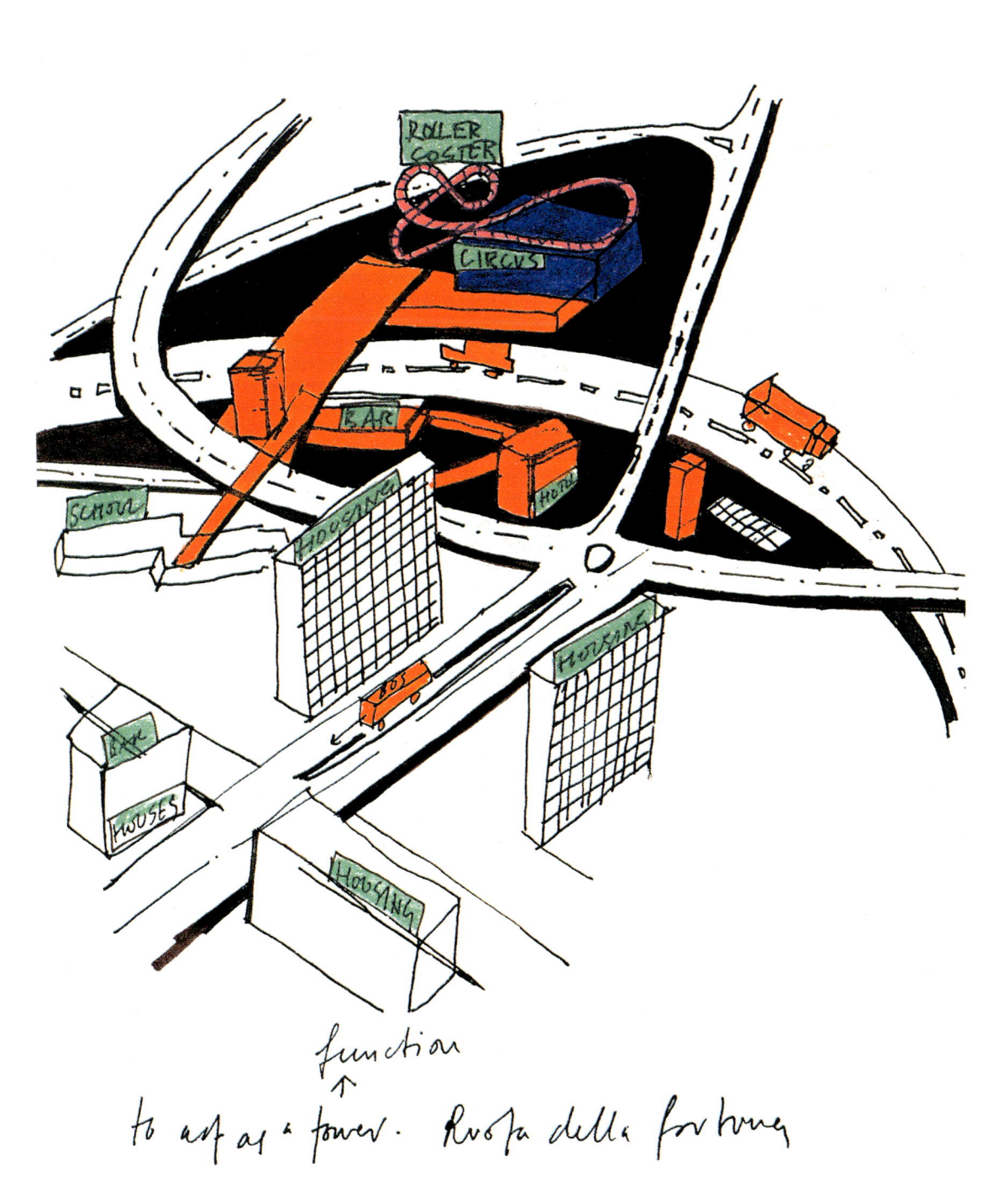

(function)

Vendor's Box

COMES INTO THE APPARTMEN...

A LIGHT BULB IN THE DARK
CAN NOT SHOW ITSELF WITHOUT
SHOWING YOU SOMETHING ELSE TOO.
- PUT IT INTO A BOX.

N° 69

@ · FOLLOW ME BECOMES
FOLLOW THE BOX,
RATHER
FIND THE BOX.

④ FIVE BIG HANDKERCH...
FOR A POUND.

THE BRIXTON ③ THE UNCANNY.
BOX COLUMN. BOX

DIMENSIONS: 40 X 85 X 40 cm

The materials of the box are fibreglass and aluminium. The design criteria were lightness and transformability – the box had to be assembled and dismantled in the time it takes an underground train's doors to open and close.

The box opens by applied pressure to the underside. Two countersunk sprung locks are fitted to the inner fibreglass casing which also acts as a table leg, connecting the fibreglass leg to a separate aluminium box section. The hinges were manufactured from solid aluminium blocks using both milling and CNC machinery.

1. walk

2. select a place to set up

3. set up the box

4. done

18 On Certain Possibilities for the Irrational Embellishment of a Town Ten Urban Artefacts

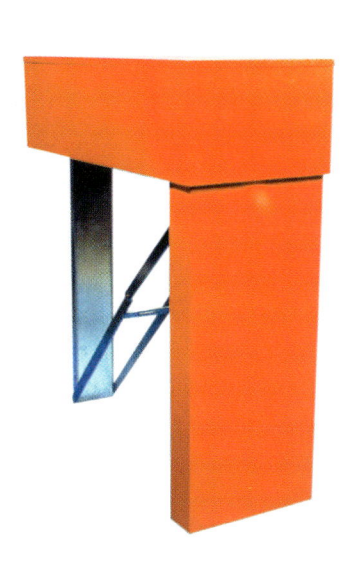

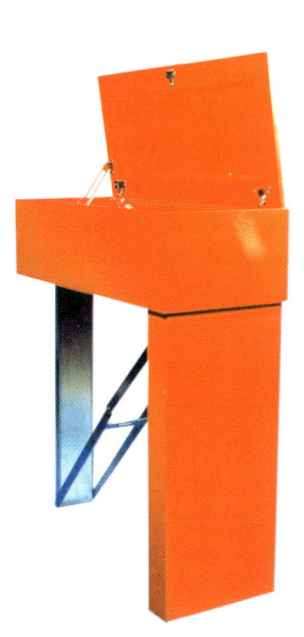

Vendor's Box

$a + \cancel{5} \sqrt{a^6 - a} \quad \sqrt{a^5 \cdot (a-1)^2} = \vert a$

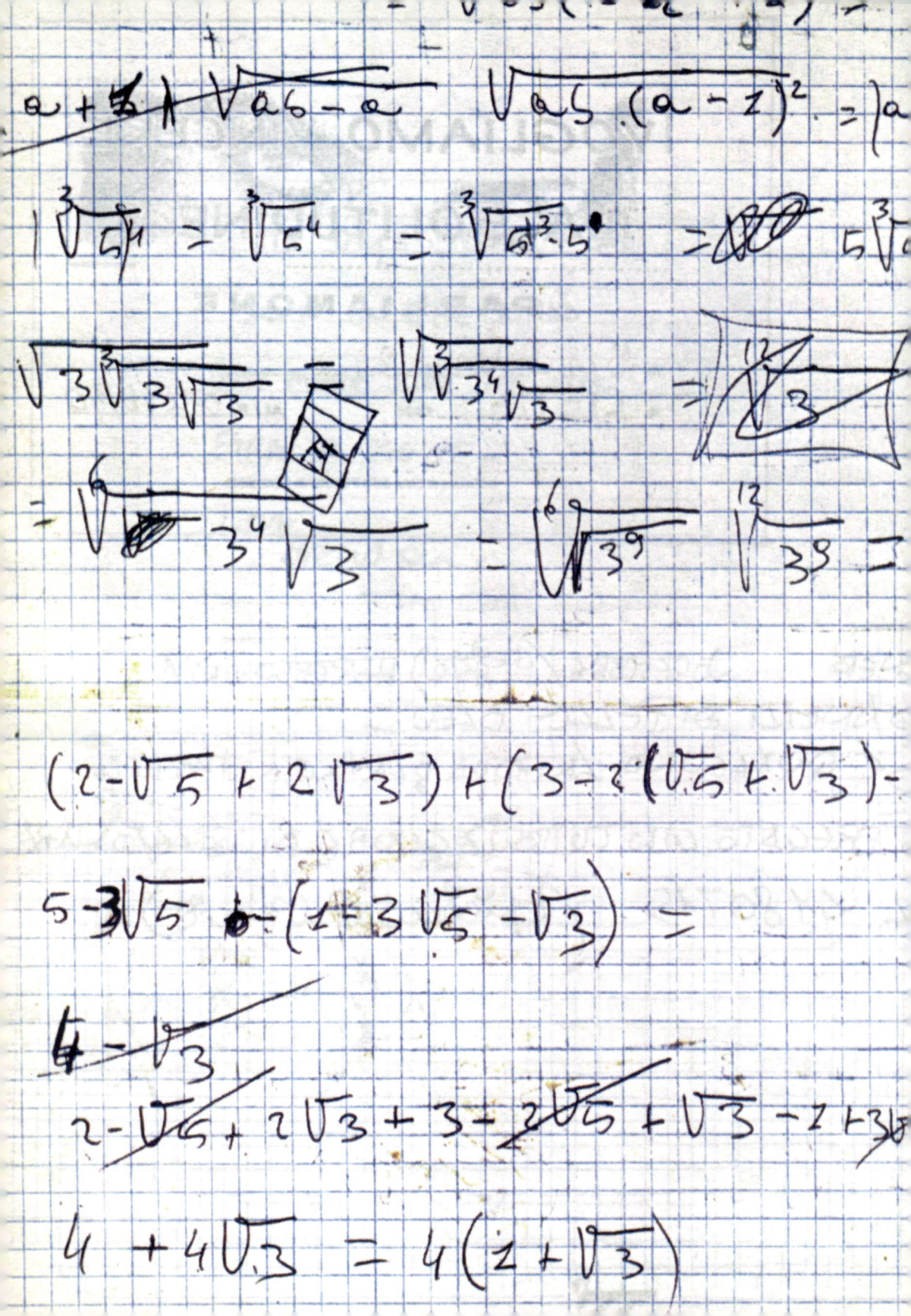

$\sqrt[3]{5^4} = \sqrt[3]{5^4} = \sqrt[3]{5^3 \cdot 5} = \cancel{\sqrt[3]{5}} \; 5\sqrt[3]{a}$

$\sqrt{3\sqrt[3]{3\sqrt{3}}} = \sqrt[3]{\sqrt{3^4\sqrt{3}}} = \cancel{\sqrt[12]{3}}$

$= \sqrt{\sqrt[3]{3^4\sqrt{3}}} = \sqrt[6]{\sqrt{3^9}} = \sqrt[12]{3^9} =$

$(2 - \sqrt{5} + 2\sqrt{3}) + (3 - ?(\sqrt{5} + \sqrt{3}) -$

$5 - 3\sqrt{5} - (1 + 3\sqrt{5} - \sqrt{3}) =$

$4 - \sqrt{3}$

$2 - \sqrt{5} + 2\sqrt{3} + 3 - 2\sqrt{5} + \sqrt{3} - 1 + 3\sqrt{3}$

$4 + 4\sqrt{3} = 4(1 + \sqrt{3})$

Writing Booth – Tom Emerson

Tom was a recent arrival in Cambridge, an émigré from the exotic formalism developing at the Royal College of Art. At the time he was preoccupied by two particular influences. The first was the writing of Georges Perec. It was Perec's obsession with formal virtuosity within self-imposed constraints that he found had a direct resonance with his thoughts about design and fabrication. The second was the work of Adalberto Libera, within the context and contradictions of modernism and civic representation in Fascist Italy. These themes were drawn together in Tom's scrapbook of his journey to EUR and Rome. At the opening of this he quoted Perec and two years later, reviewing a newly translated edition of Perec's *Species of Spaces* he wrote:

> Perec employs a rigorous structure of ascending scales, devoting each chapter to separate species of space, one fitting inside the next like a Russian doll. The first chapter is devoted to the space of the page, within which the book is written, as if space can only be discussed or described once the co-ordinates upon which this is done have been given. Then follow chapters on the bed, the bedroom, the flat, the building, the neighbourhood, the city, the countryside, the country, Europe, the Old Continent, the New Continent, the world and space.

Wanting to derive his work from Perec's notion of the space of the page and the written word, he researched writing devices and began by investigating the letter's journey, posting to himself a parcel containing a movement-sensitive tape recorder. The result was an exquisite record of the mundane passage of his parcel from the letter box to the postal van via sorting office conversations, rapid handling, to the return and deposit at his front door.

After a failed attempt to work within the impossibly restrictive dimensions of a door leaf, he began to envisage furniture that would create an island of personal space within a public space to enable the act of writing in these circumstances – an object that would both create and contain space.

The *Writing Booth* developed through a series of permutations from a single cell to the tenser economy of the back to back version. The idea that this double unit could either stand alone, or in line or, at its densest, as a series of offset units, developed alongside the three-and-a-half sided plan. Tom developed an alternative for either a standing/leaning or sitting/kneeling configuration of seat and tablet to reflect different durations of occupancy, comfort and preferred perspectives. In order that it was perceived as furniture and not a fitted architectural element, and to create a psychological threshold, the floor was raised 100mm off the finished floor level of the public space.

To maintain a reasonable but tight dimension, both the writing tablet and the seat are angled. The tablet made of solid aluminium with a groove for holding a writing implement is rolled to tilt the writing plane gently from the horizontal. The seat or resting plane is angled more steeply to an orthopaedic and ergonomic position. These two solid metal elements are also used to 'lock' and stabilise the sides of the booth, as is the raised floor plane.

In its elemental form, Tom wanted to create an object that was intentionally neutral and ambiguous – not a table and chair, but possibly a urinal or confessional, possibly packaging or nothing useful at all. The process veered between the purely sculptural and material – solid sheets of aluminium or steel – to the pragmatics of furniture and economic constraint. At the same time, alternatives for the method of fabrication – the mechanisation of mass production or the highly crafted object – offered another means to tune the quality of the piece in its intended setting. There was a desire that the booth would be sited in the hard chequered terrazzo floors associated with post offices of the post-war period – echoes also of the extraordinary quality of natural light and shadow in Libera's Post Office at EUR. The material quality of the interior of this building is also evident in the exterior, which, at a distance, gives the impression of a massive sculptured continuum, but which at close quarters offers up its finely crafted thin bed stone work.

Writing Booth

24   **On Certain Possibilities for the Irrational Embellishment of a Town** Ten Urban Artefacts

The analysis of precedent raised the twin questions of materiality and fabrication, a common ground between architecture, furniture, sculpture and a fundamental part of the broader questions of representation and physiognomy. The different emphasis that a sculptor will place on issues like authorship, constraint, programme or presence shed a new, sometimes dazzling, light on assumed perceptions in the other two fields and vice versa. As an image unfettered by the issues of moveability, storage (or flat pack assembly), adaptability, reconfiguration, and wear and tear that may be the first question a furniture designer will ask, Tom's object desire had an overt echo of Donald Judd's permanent installation of one hundred works in the artillery sheds at Marfa. There strong side light pours over the milled aluminium furniture scaled pieces, creating an interplay of fragmented reflective planes that suggest a weightless dematerialisation of solid and void within the mute simplicity of the screed floor and the pragmatic concrete soffit of beams and slab. The *Writing Booth* puts an ambiguous spatial cloak around Antonello Da Messina's *St Jerome*, and aids the act of writing in a minimal cell of tranquillity within the public sphere. The early graphite rendering of the dull reflectivity of milled aluminium gave way to experiments with the material itself and the question of finish either as the surface of an unstable thin veneer or the manifestation of thick self-supporting slab stock. Richard Serra articulated the difference of perception between container and contained and the question of fabrication in architecture and sculpture in a recent interview with David Sylvester about the installation of his series of *Torqued Ellipses*, at the Guggenheim Museum in Bilbao:

I still think that they work better in relationship to straight vertical walls than to curvilinear walls and ceilings. The curvilinear architecture and its busy baroqueness detract from the exterior volumes of the sculptures. In the ellipses you have the outside of the outside, and then you have the inside of the outside on the outside, and then you have the inside of the inside, and then again you have the outside of the inside on the inside. These pieces continuously ask you to pay attention to their surface as it moves from what you would think is an interior form to an exterior form. In some way they become topologically continuous. That continuity breaks if you start relating them to the rhythms of curvilinear walls and ceilings. Also, the curvilinearity of this room is a little soft, a little like cheesecake. If anything, the precision of the *Torqued Ellipses* points to the shoddiness of the drawing in the architecture. The detailing of the sheet-rock is shabby.

Tom, questioning the appropriate density of the materiality of the booth, began to work with a stiff timber core overclad with a minimum thickness of sheet aluminium. Driven by economics, metal sheet size and an intrigue with issues of cladding, he worked on the lightness of a panel and how the booth could be assembled from a flat pack, using the low grade technology of industrialised kitchen cabinets rather than the hi-tech precision of computer controlled joining and cutting technology. Working with 0.8mm sheet bonded to all sides of an 18mm MDF core he developed an obsession with the tolerance of butted surfaces to create a reliable, smooth and precise finish. These, like the controlled evidence of masonry corner details can be used, as in a bird's beak joint, the lapping joints of load bearing masonry or the continuous joint of the veneer, to conceal or emphasise thinness. To create the strength of bond between these materials an impact adhesive was used that offered no adjustment and necessitated the construction of a jig to allow the two surfaces to meet in perfect uniformity.

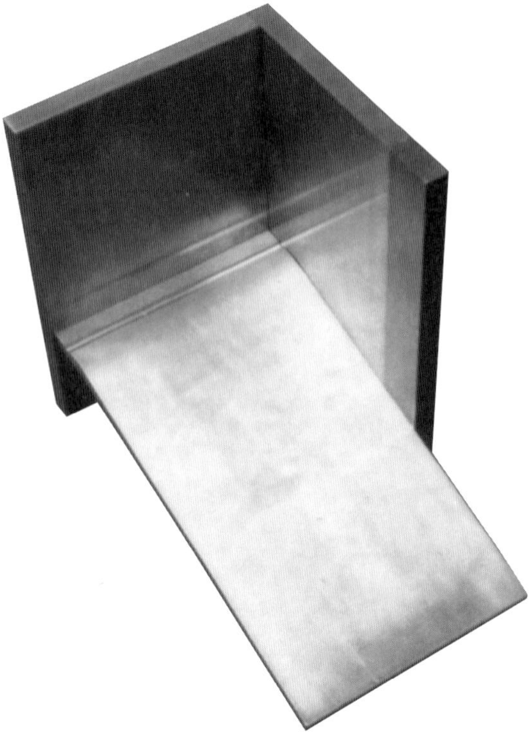

Il y a peu d'événements qui ne laissent au moins une trace écrite. Presque tout, à un moment ou à un autre, passe par une feuille de papier, une page de carner, un feuillet d'agenda ou n'importe quel autre support de fortune (un ticket de métro, une marge de journal, un paquet de cigarettes, le dos d'une enveloppe, etc.) sur lequel vient s'inscrire, à une vitesse variable et selon des techniques différentes selon le lieu, l'heure ou l'humeur, l'un ou l'autre des divers éléments qui composent l'ordinaire de la vie.

georges perec
espèces d'espaces

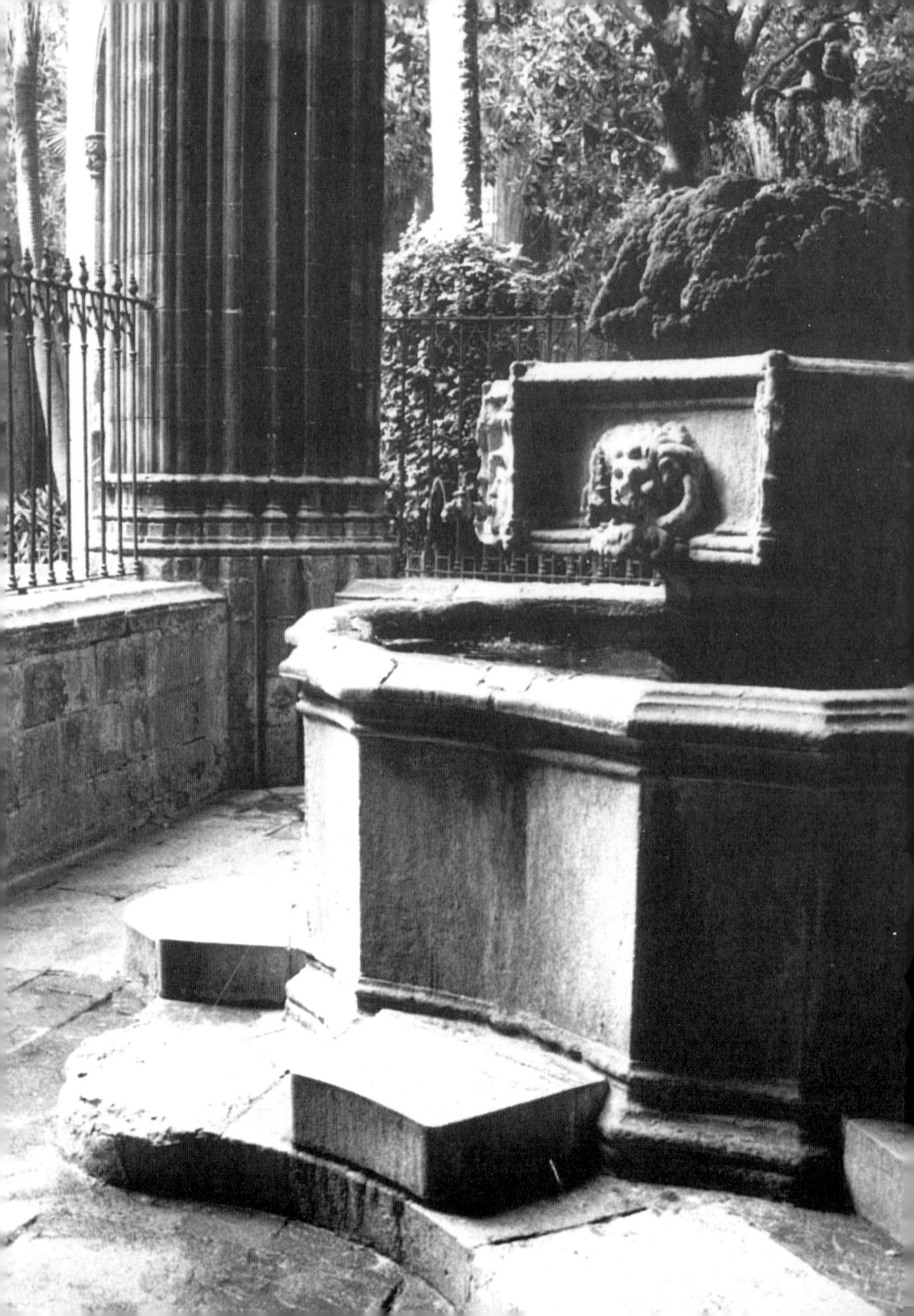

Spring – Nicholas Zervoglos

The development of the ability to discard and jettison stillborn ideas and to enter into a creative 'cycle of failure' leading in an uneven spiral towards a focused end is an essential initiation common to all fields of design.

Spring is now a millennium product, but one term into the project, at the end of January 1996, two e-mails illustrate the beginning of its precarious passage:

Date: Thu, 1 Feb 1996 11:50:50 +0000 (GMY)

From "c.Y.Barlow" cyb1@eng.cam.ac.uk

To "N.Zervoglos" nz201@hermes.cam.ac.uk

Subject: Re: that fountain again

On Wed, 31 Jan 1996, N Zervoglos wrote:

> I am wondering whether it is practical to make a sheet less than 1mm

> thick out of fibre glass.

> Yes, you can make it thin, but I don't think it would be rigid or

tough enough.

> How thin could one make it, and yet still have

> it somewhat resistant to vandalism? Would kevlar help? (I understand it

> is not very rigid and yet is knife proof).

I think you had better try your experiment. Kevlar would make it

more resistant to vandals, certainly

> If you don't think there is a straight forward answer to my question, I

> can set up a little experiment and test samples.

>

> What difficult questions you do ask!

> CYB

Date: Thu, 1 Feb 1996 13:32:548 +0000 (GMY)

From "A.Harte" ah10013@hermes.cam.ac.uk

To "N.Zervoglos" nz201@hermes.cam.ac.uk

Subject: rubber for matrix

The regime that has been used on the braids that you saw goes like this.

1. Pyratex 240
made by Bayer
gives a sticky rubber

2. Revenex 840 99 parts
Beetle BE338 1 part
Revenex sold by Doverstrand
Beetle sold by BIP Chemicals limited

– gives drier feel to the surface without affecting inner rubber

If you want more info I have all of the data sheets and curing schedules. The person who passed all of this on to me is R. Woods in physiology. His number is 33845 but he is quite difficult to get hold of. Your best bet is faxing him at the physiology department at 33840.

On Certain Possibilities for the Irrational Embellishment of a Town Ten Urban Artefacts

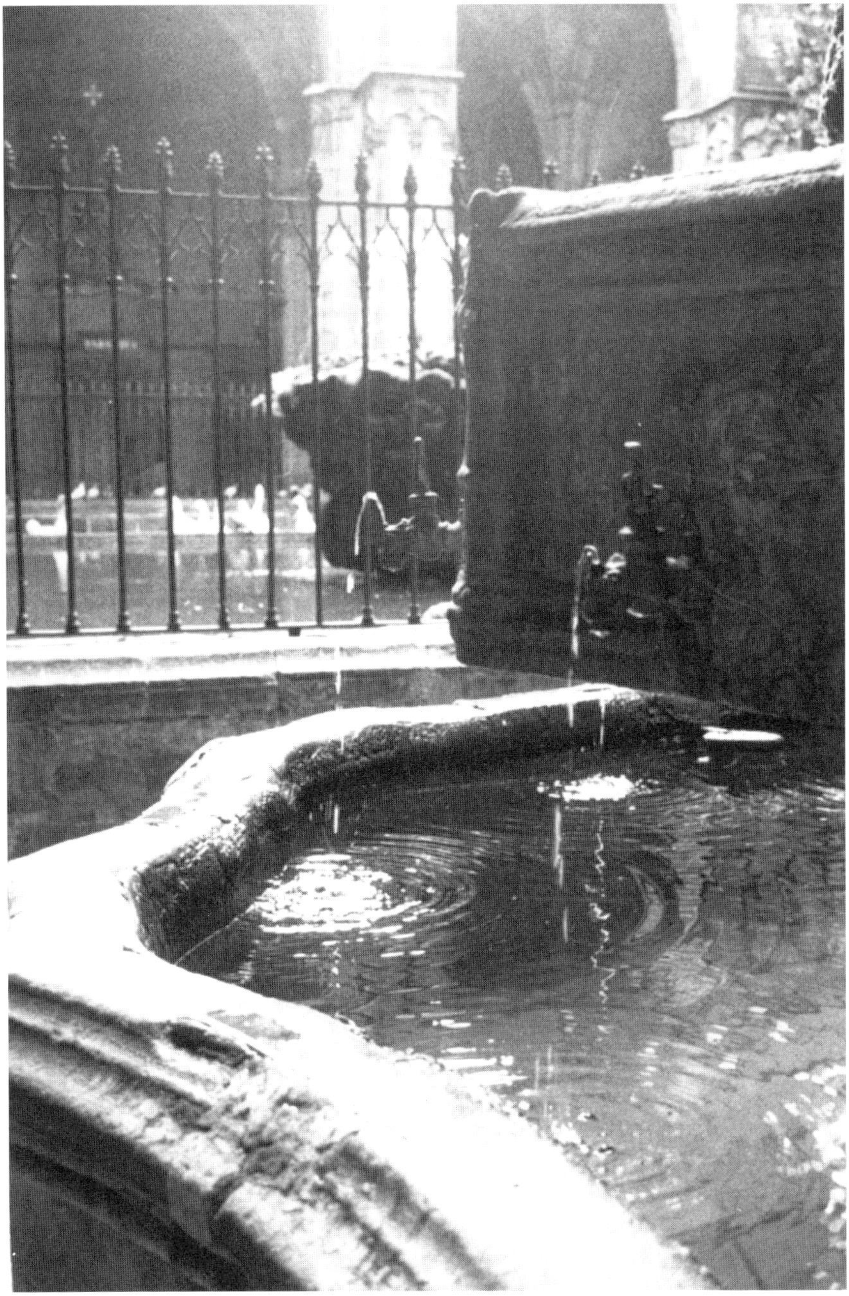

On Certain Possibilities for the Irrational Embellishment of a Town Ten Urban Artefacts

Spring 33

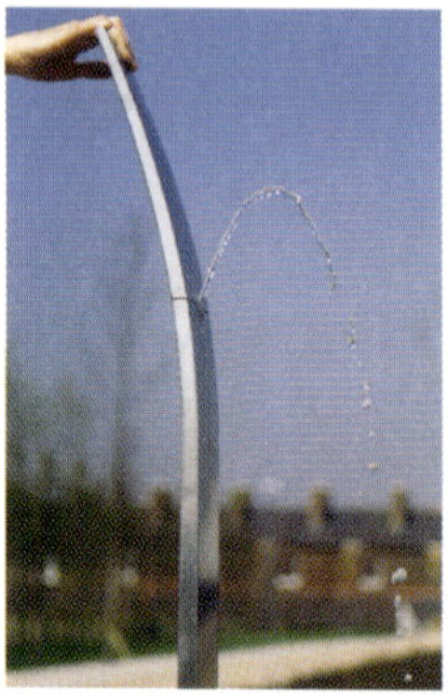

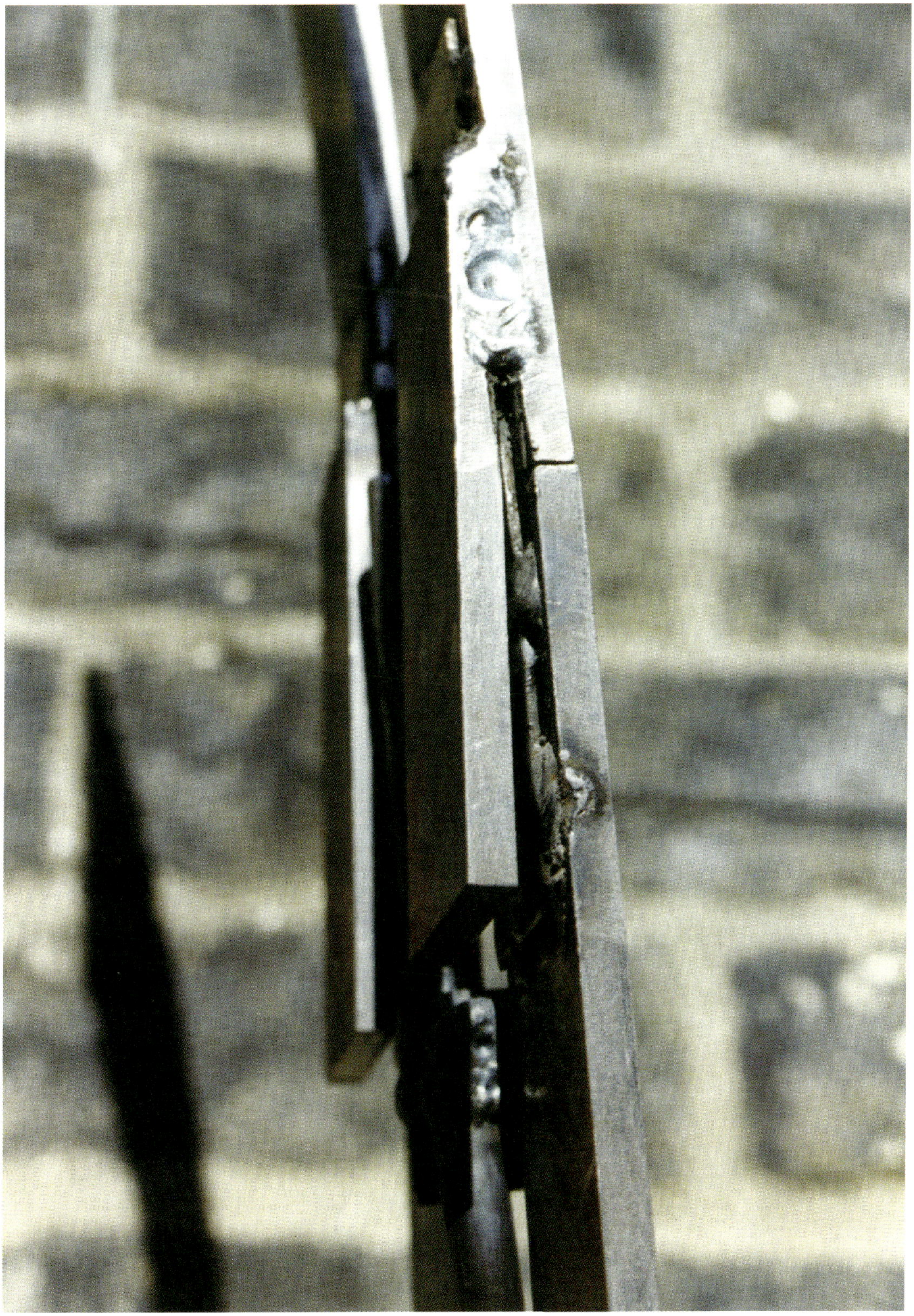

On Certain Possibilities for the Irrational Embellishment of a Town Ten Urban Artefacts

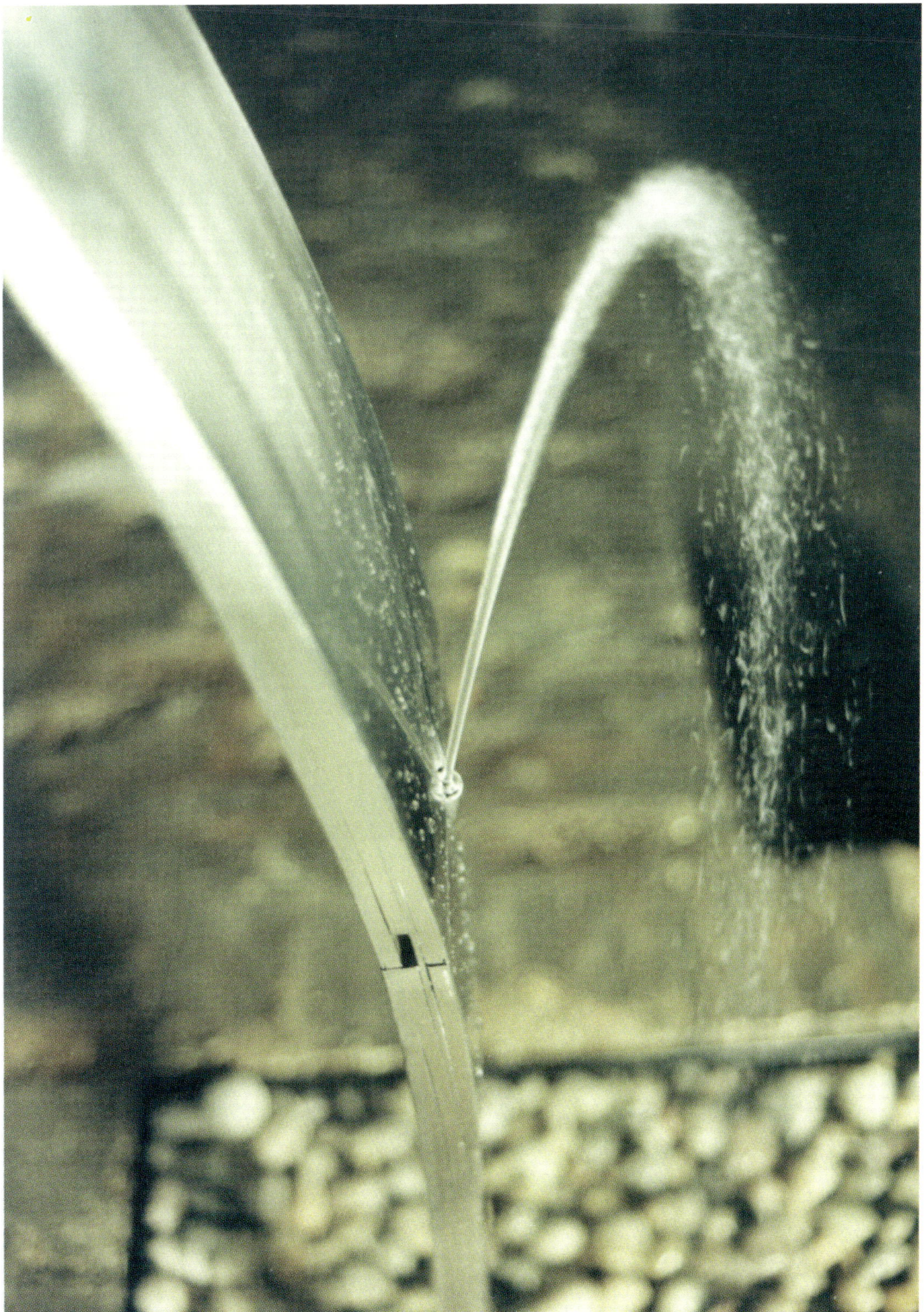

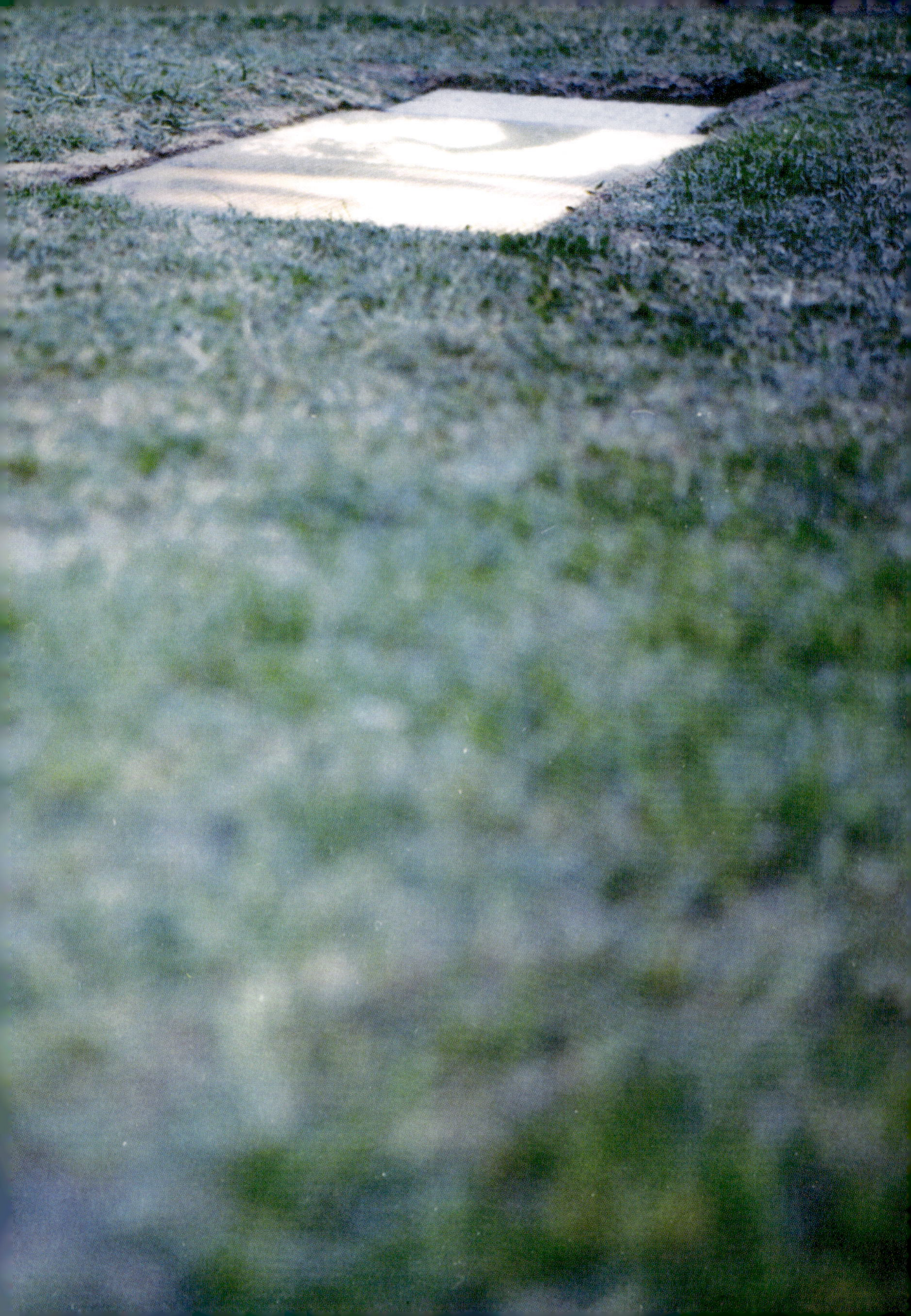

Pavement Lights – Ben Adams

Arguably the most pervasive element of the city, and particularly the public realm is the nature of its horizontal external surfaces. The number of people affected by its character is exponentially greater than that of even its busiest transport interchange. It is the unspoken, unassuming but shared medium through which the population of a city corresponds. Remove all other traces and hints of place from a photograph of a street and the detail of junctions and materials will offer a potent clue, like a genetic fingerprint, of which city, with all its complex cultural make-up, you are looking at. Archaeologists resurrect complete forms from the stratigraphic concentrate of ruins crushed into the surface of the earth. Artists conjure situations out of the palest recordings of a city's landscape.

To justify this myopic belief, it may be helpful to draw upon some explicit examples. Lisbon and, in particular, the Baixa – the lower town rebuilt on the ancient silt beds and rubble after the earthquake of 1755 – is characterised by the *opus sectile* of black and white granite squares laid, as a standard, in flowing patterns and simple repetitive geometries in the principal streets and squares. Try, in you minds eye, changing this dominant grey-white surface, the lightness and reflectivity of which tends to levitate the abutting limestone buildings by diminishing the shadows of rustication and cills, with the sombre, abrasive and absorbent York stone of London's pavements. The result is perplexing, all the more because both the buildings and the pavement of each are familiar in their own context, but drawn together act like the incoherent juxtapositions of a personalised virtual world.

The streets of Prague have a sophisticated modulation of scale between the tight grain and smaller scale of the pavement and the coarser setts of the carriageway. Both are compressed to their boundaries by two or three rows of setts laid perpendicular to the adjacent edge acting like the springing to a centred flat arch and create a formal border between building, pavement and granite kerb. This is a time honoured convention, a base from which to develop different nuances as, for instance, in the wall of an institution with no pavement or in the bands of tonally differentiated material marking inclines and changes of direction. It is the order, elaborate as it is, of the ordinary onto which is grafted the special quality of particular places – the giant scale of the paving blocks of the Cour d'honneur of Prague Castle or the more formal grid of Josip Plecnik's Third courtyard repaving.

On Certain Possibilities for the Irrational Embellishment of a Town Ten Urban Artefacts

Pavement Lights

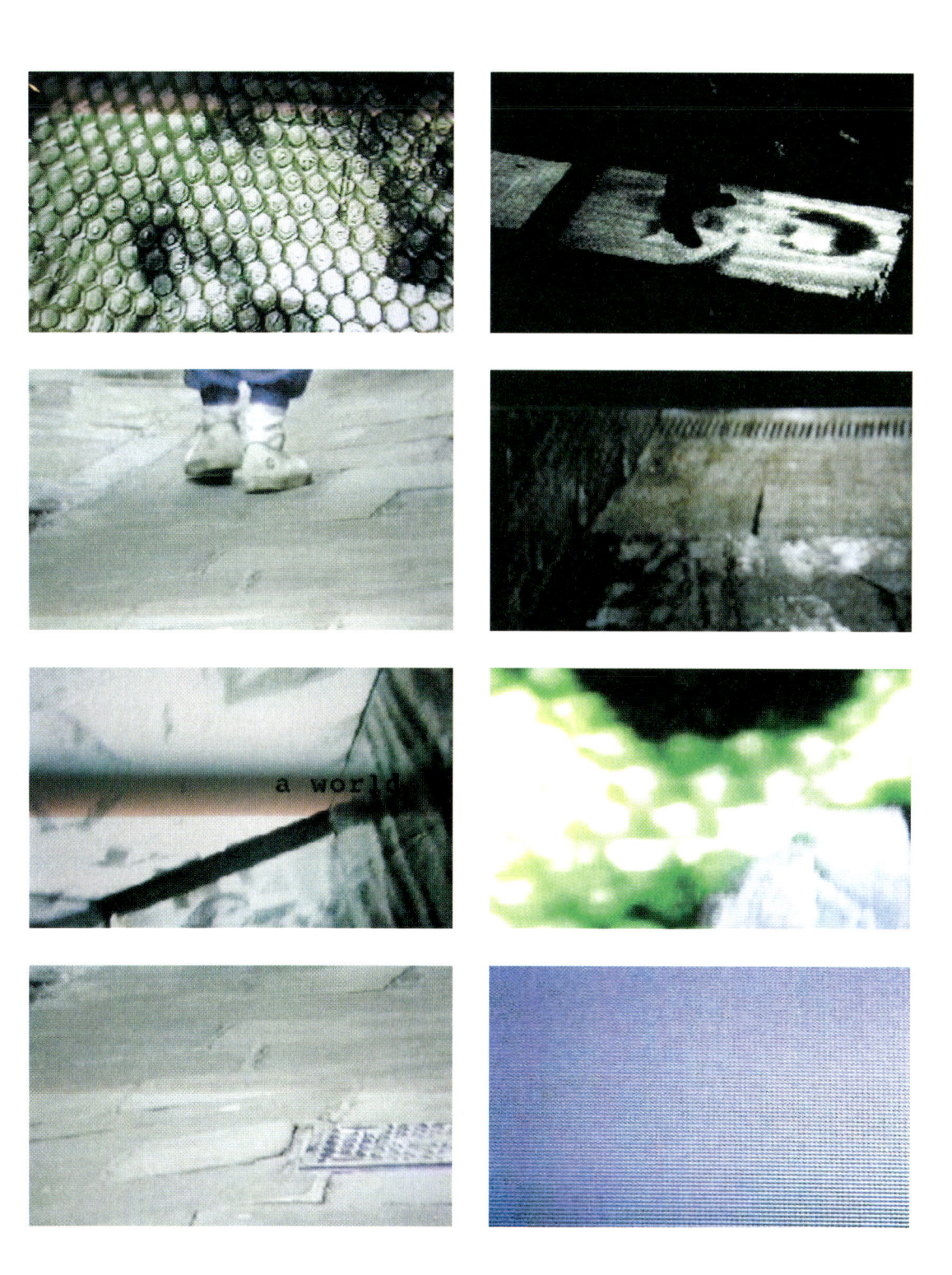

42 On Certain Possibilities for the Irrational Embellishment of a Town Ten Urban Artefacts

Pavement Lights

AGE
SPACE

Borderline – David Grandorge

David Grandorge has developed his interests in a number of ways besides practising architecture, most notably as a talented photographer. He also has the generosity of spirit to be, even when pressed, helpful to others and the brief for *Borderline* grew out of a commitment to working with youth groups in North West London as a football coach. He chose as a setting a specific context – Lonsdale Road NW6 – and began by recording its street elevations in a photographic survey. This area is squeezed between the trajectory of railway tracks and a series of open spaces, some the result of Victorian urban cleansing, including Wormwood Scrubs and the parkland cemeteries of Kensal Green and Willesden Lane. The latter forms the northern boundary to Lonsdale Road which is characterised by an unusual conjunction of domestic terraced housing and light industrial workshops. It is also a popular thoroughfare for local residents and schoolchildren who are attracted to the lively and somewhat edgy quality of workshop life that spills out onto the road at regular intervals. David took two frontages and replaced the decaying solid timber workshop doors with a series of pivoting doors that both enabled degrees of openness but also, because of their framed construction and translucent sheeting, allowed a visual of connection between inside and out by day and night.

PADDINGTON M
ROAD SPRINGS COLL

The North West Group
20-26 Lonsdale Road
London, N.W.6 6RD
Tel. 071-625 7862

IMPERIAL MATCH

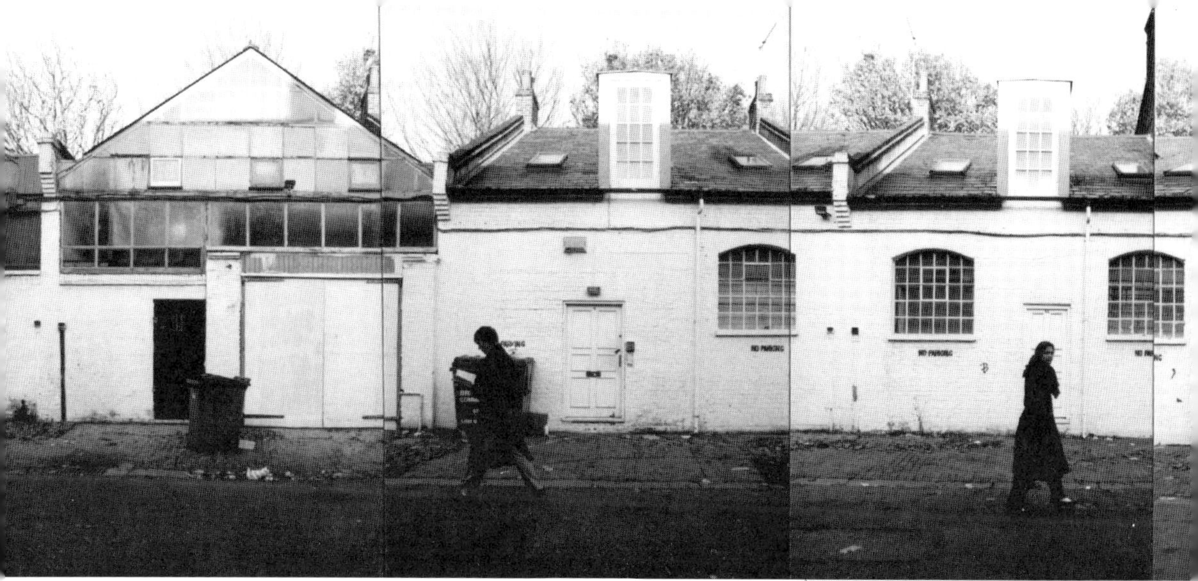

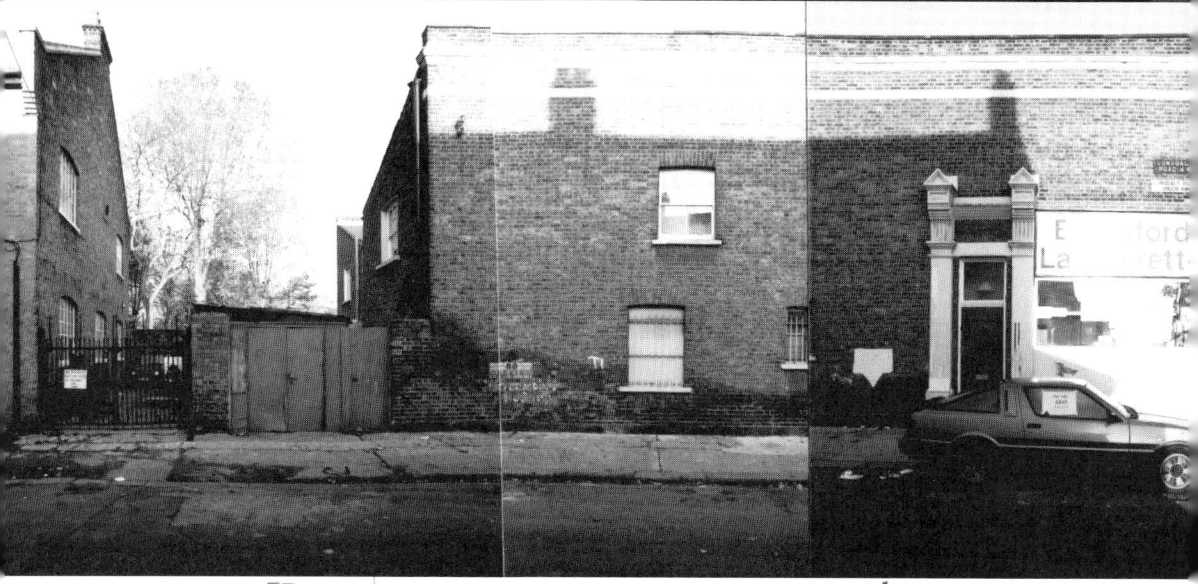

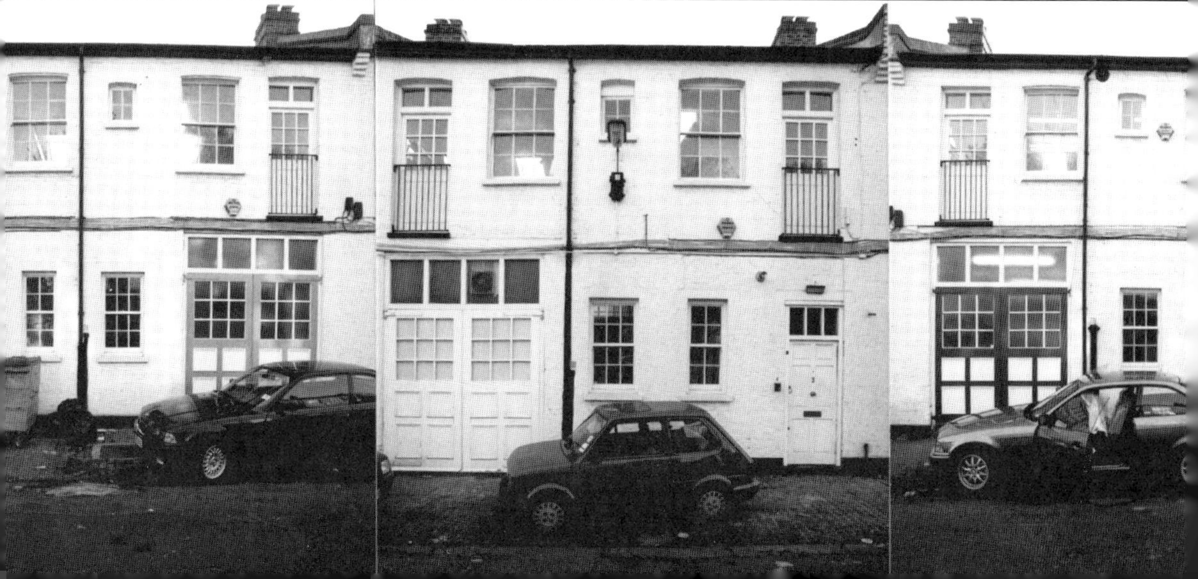

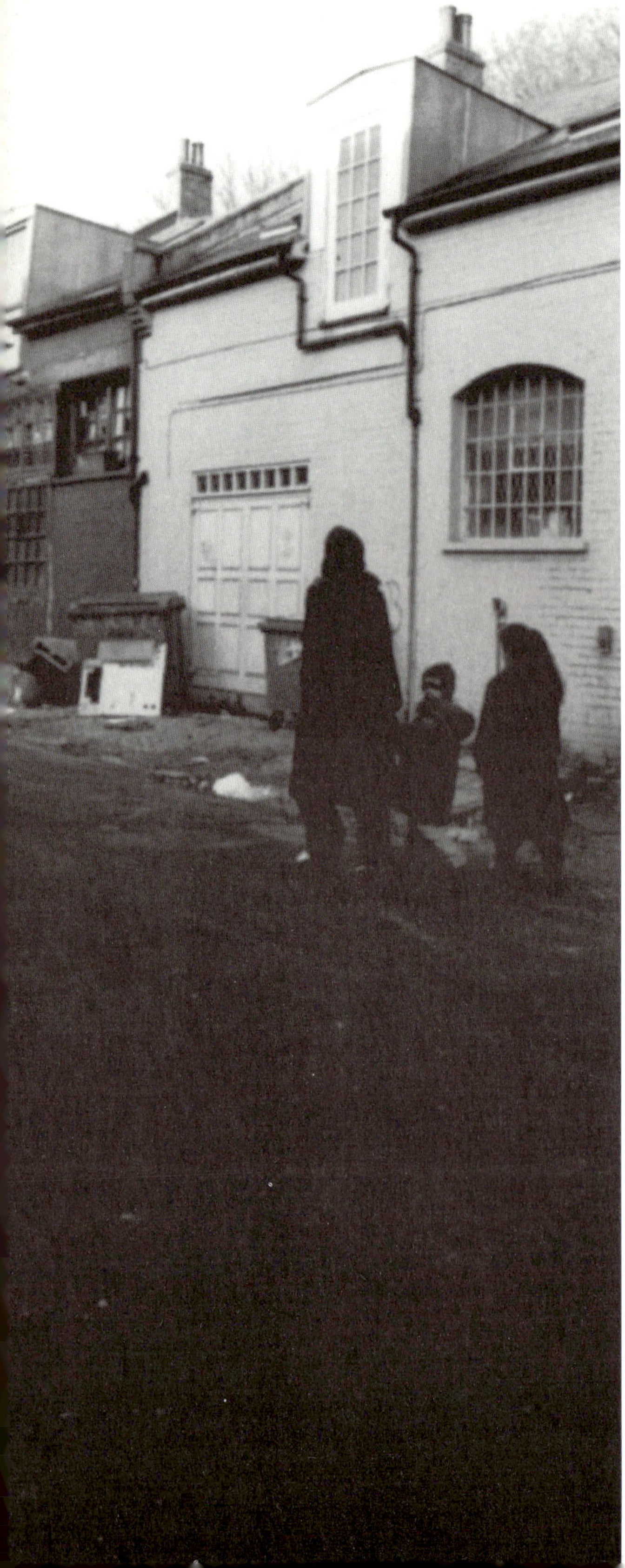

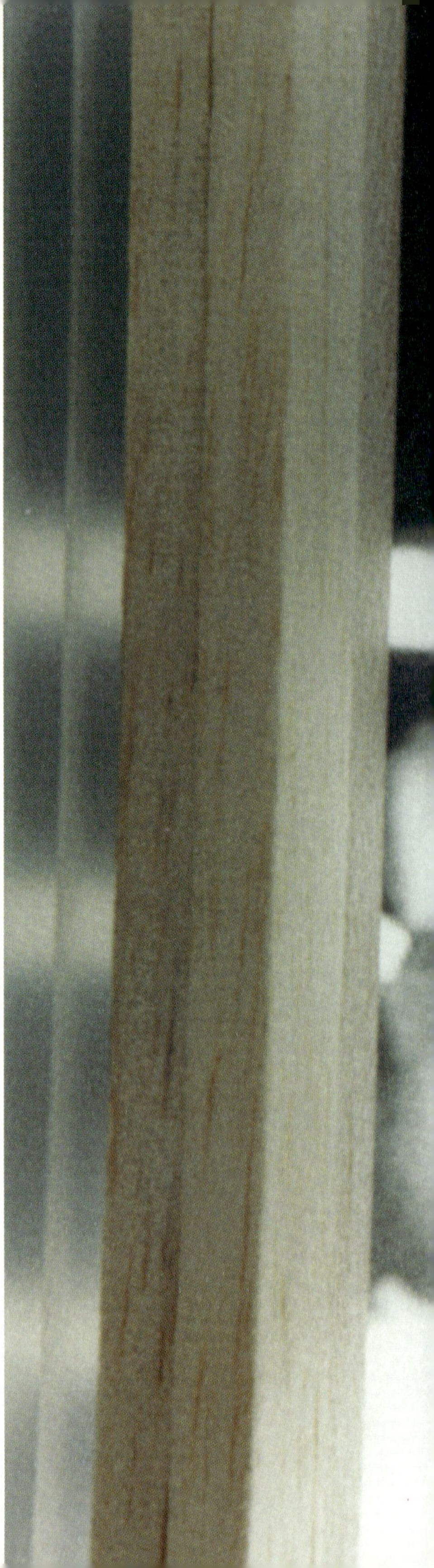

Borderline

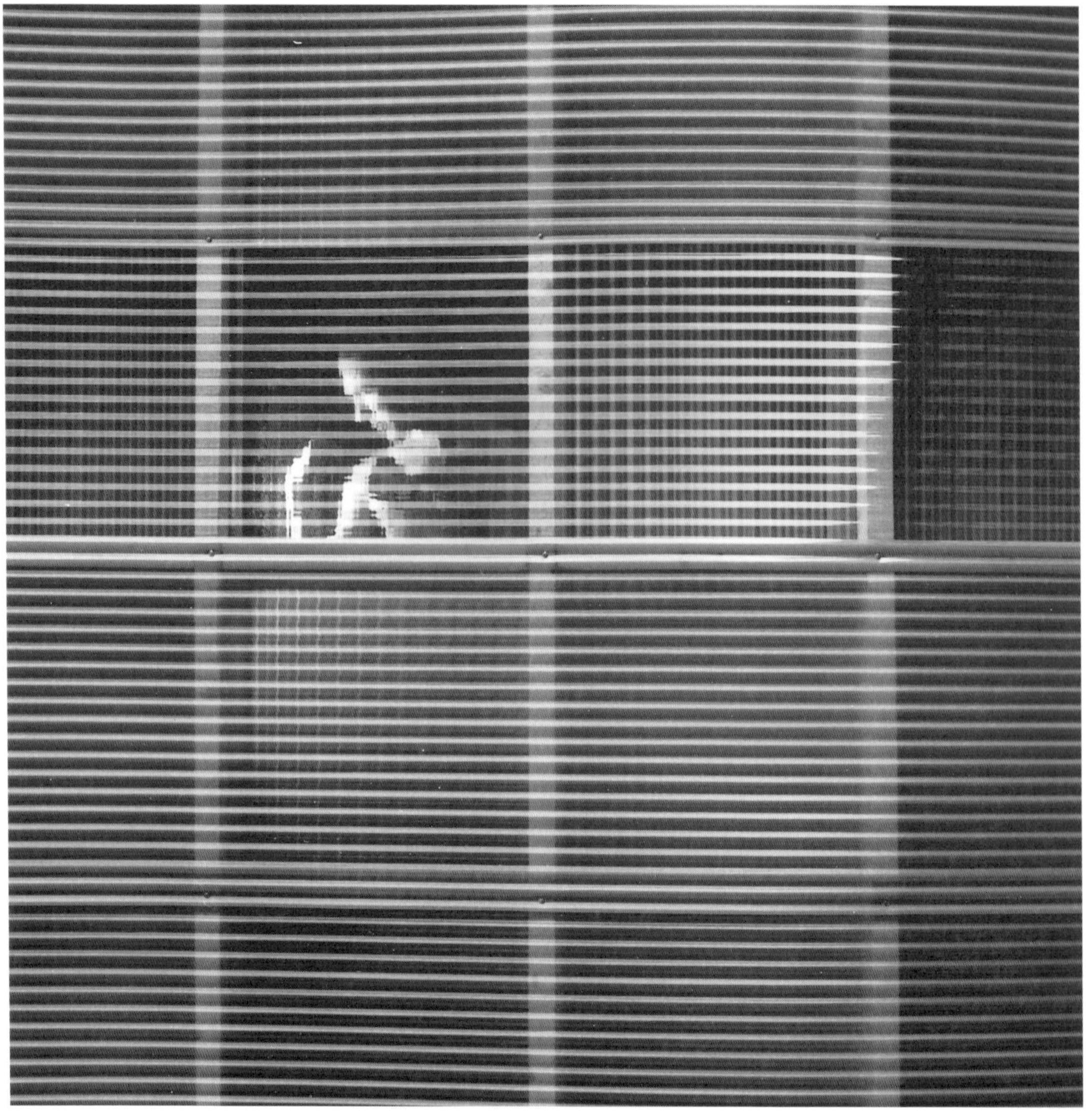

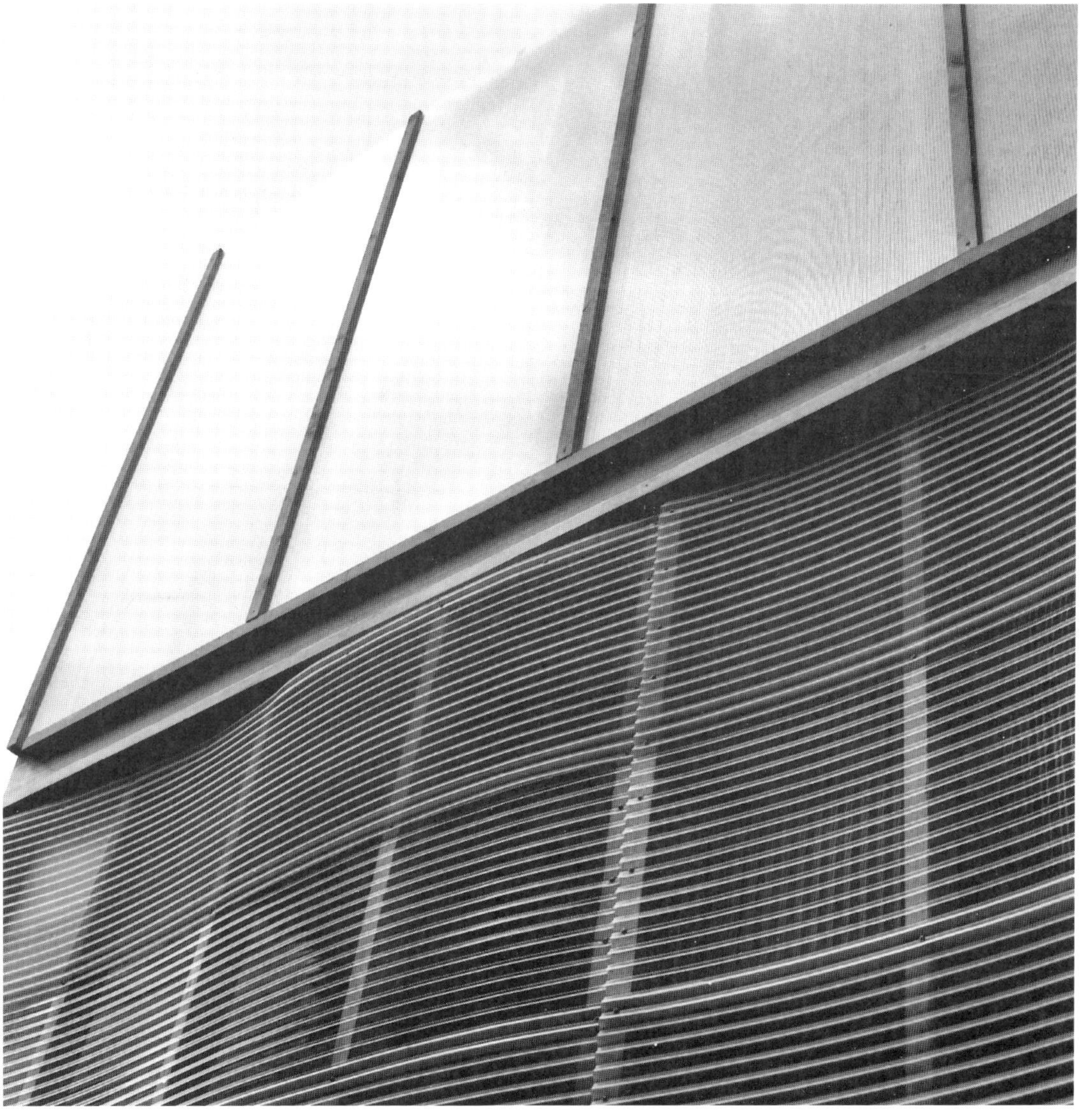

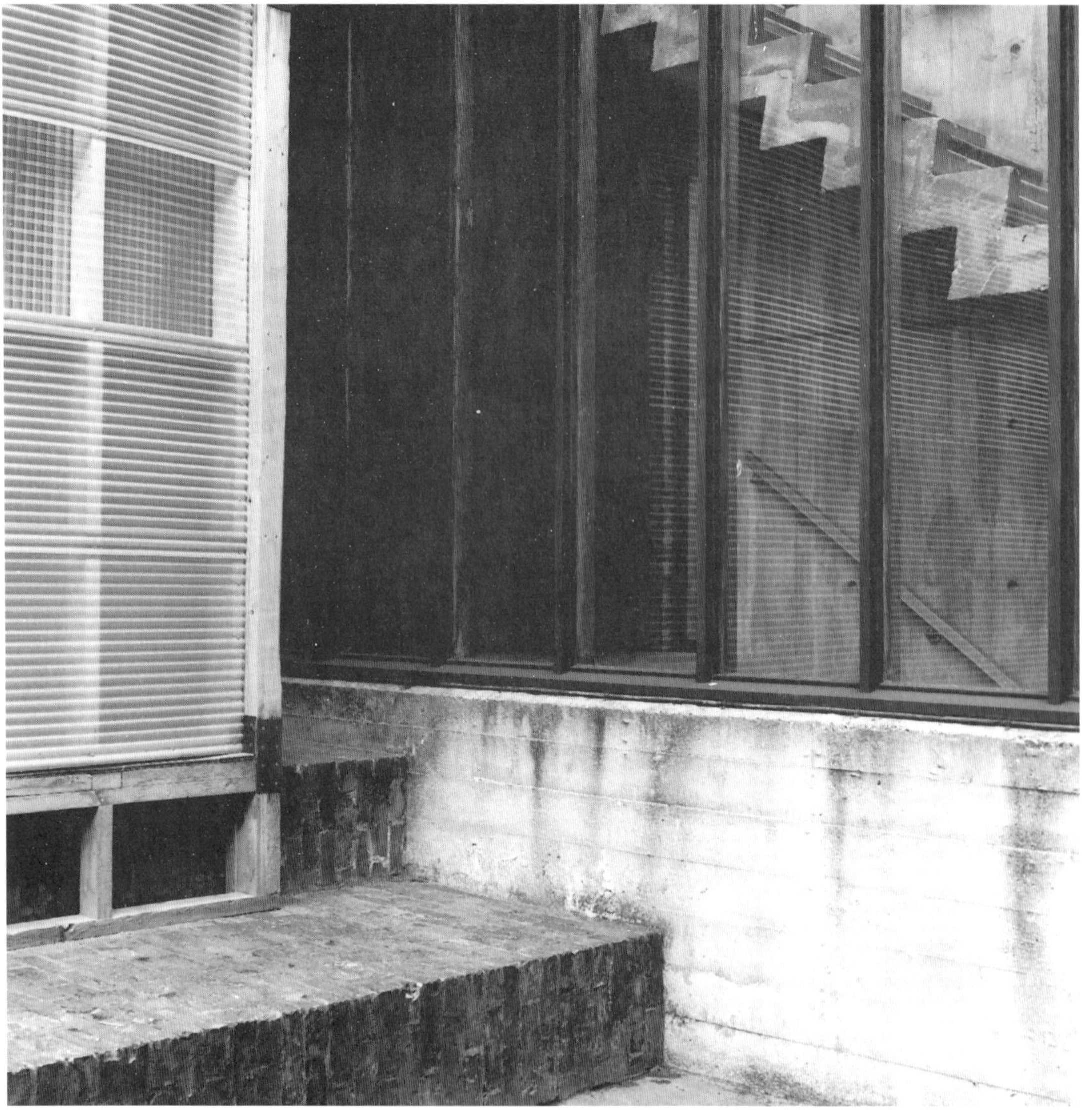

The framing was made from reclaimed timber and the sheet material – a combination of twinwall and translucent and transparent corrugated plastic – was chosen to achieve a very economical skin. The choice of materials effectively echoed the brief, which was to house a boxing gymnasium associated with a local youth club in this traditionally 'troublesome' area of London.

Borderline's location and programme touched the nerve of philanthropy and community through the underbelly of the psychology of sport as a powerful cathartic activity. Another resonance given David's work was the urban artefact as seen through the shop window – a development of one of Tom Dixon's ideas, seen in the design of his furniture and shop, space, where an LCD screen had been incorporated into a glass plane creating a tantalising animated framing of both a virtual and real condition. David's 'screen' – with its insistent ribbing and reflections enliven the pixilation of screen technology in an ironic mirror of real and imagined urban tendencies.

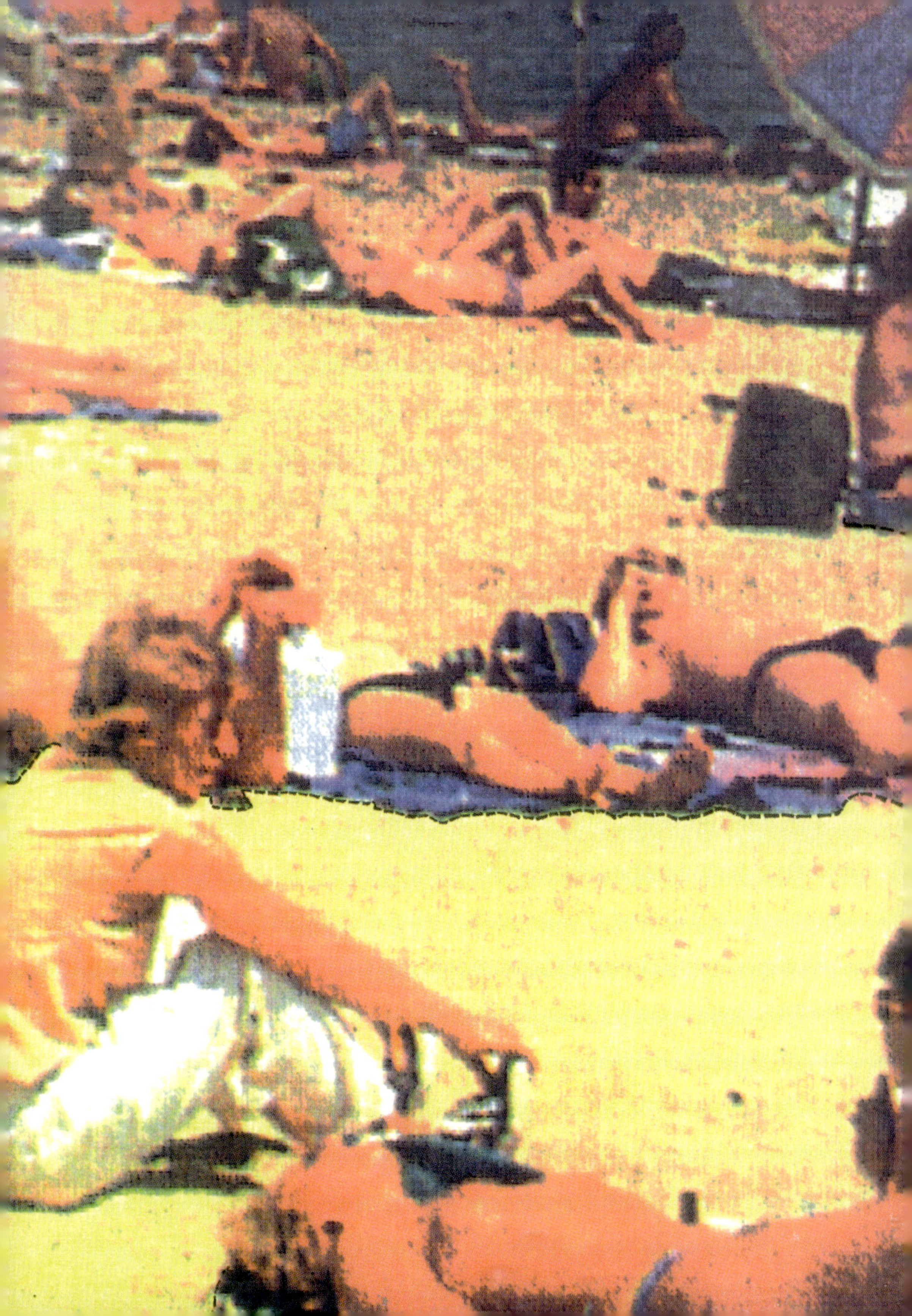

Day Bed – Emma Huckett

Emma Huckett was drawn to the issue of personal space in the public realm partly because of research she has carried out on accessibility and physical disability. She had also begun a thesis on sound and spatial recognition for the visually impaired, including the possibility of a sound map for the Underground. Her first ideas for *Day Bed* developed from an observation of social codes in contexts of public proximity, like that of an individual's towel on a beach.

Next she turned to the question of travel and used the railway station as the spatial context for her investigation. With travel comes a state of introspection and reverie – from the window of a train or plane the landscape or cloudscape becomes a cocooned and muffled reality. "Quietude," a collage from Max Ernst's *One Hundred Headless Women* eloquently describes this state and became a mental leitmotif which was taken with her as she worked with extraordinary tenacity on her *Day Bed*.

She began this process by setting out from London's Waterloo Station and completing a five day loop to Paris, Milan and Florence. At each station she stopped for long enough to record the patterns of use at different times of day and to research habits of waiting. At Waterloo, in the unintended waiting area next to the international ticket office, before passing through passport control, the prow of a luggage trolley doubled up to provide an uncomfortable seat. In Milan the awesome waiting rooms are a presage to some apocalypse where the sound of the turning of a key in a suitcase lock reverberates, shifting all eyes to one's most private endeavours. In Florence the hard openness of the station is equivalent to the covered colonnade of a busy street. Emma discovered that stations change character dramatically over the course of a day. She, thus, decided to design furniture that could respond to the extremes of slowness and fastness suggested by such changes. Her solution, ultimately, was the thin wall against which it is possible to rest briefly – the creation of a 'day bed' for longer use.

Two precedents of a very different nature are evident throughout the development of the *Day Bed*. First the formal precedent that has the elegant thinness of Poul Kjaerholm's chairs, with cane woven over a stainless steel frame. Second, the situational precedent of personal space defined within the public domain, like the medieval hospital bed in the Hotel du Dieu de Beaune.

The first sketches for the *Bed* show a leaf unfolding from a wall that then became a free standing element with two leaves unfurling to either side of a central post. It was clear from the beginning that this joint was going to be a crucial element in Emma's design. She wrote:

> I wanted a mechanism that allows the piece to transform from screen to bed in one simple, deliberate action. I also wanted a mechanism that allowed locking in both open and closed states – it has to enable the bed to stand upright as a screen without additional support and to lock in the bed position and permit the headrest to cantilever out.

56 **On Certain Possibilities for the Irrational Embellishment of a Town** Ten Urban Artefacts

Day Bed   57

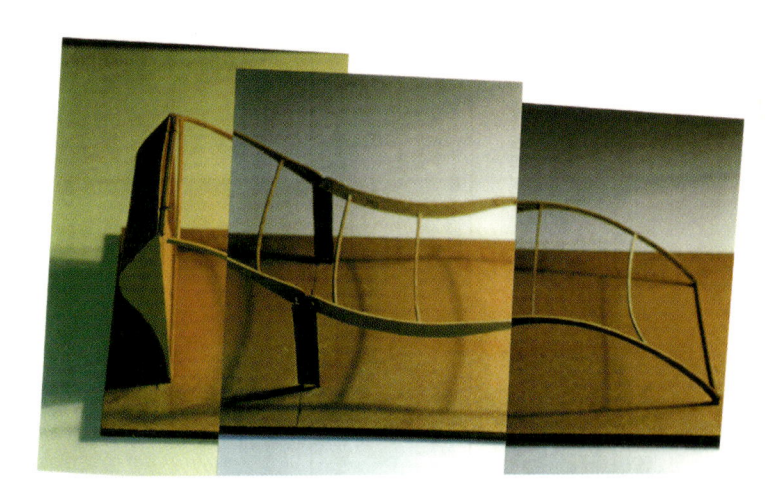

58 **On Certain Possibilities for the Irrational Embellishment of a Town** Ten Urban Artefacts

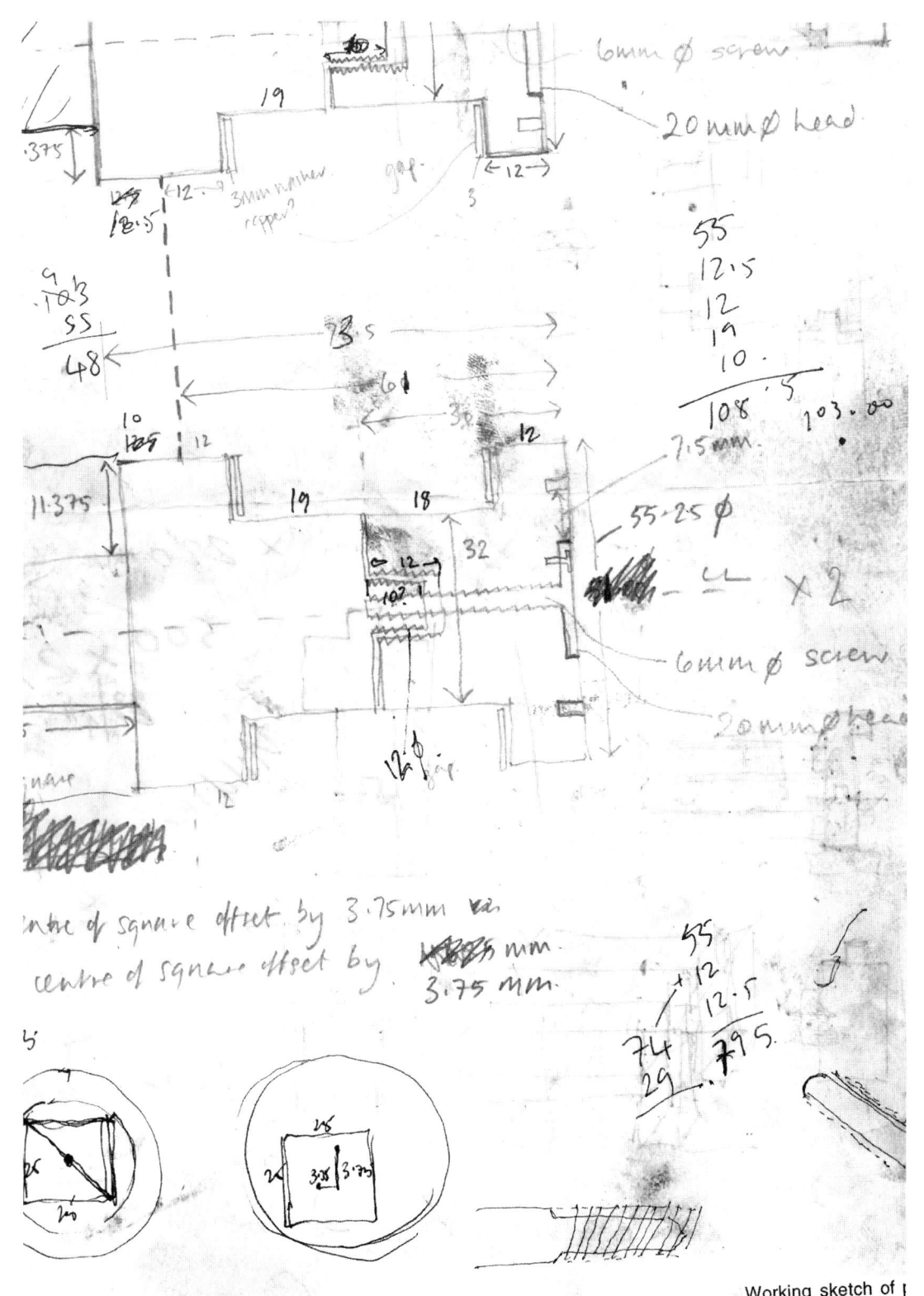

Working sketch of

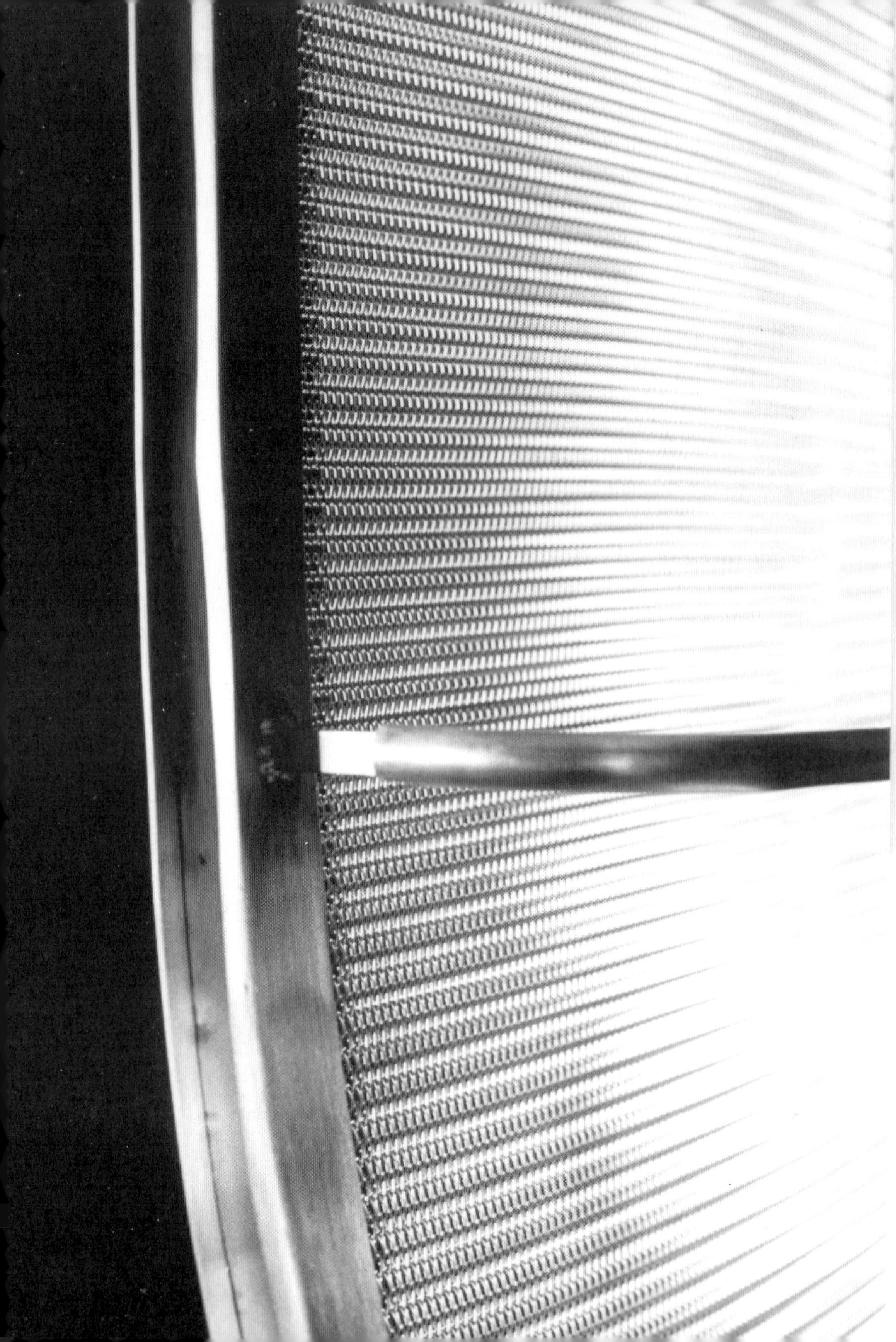

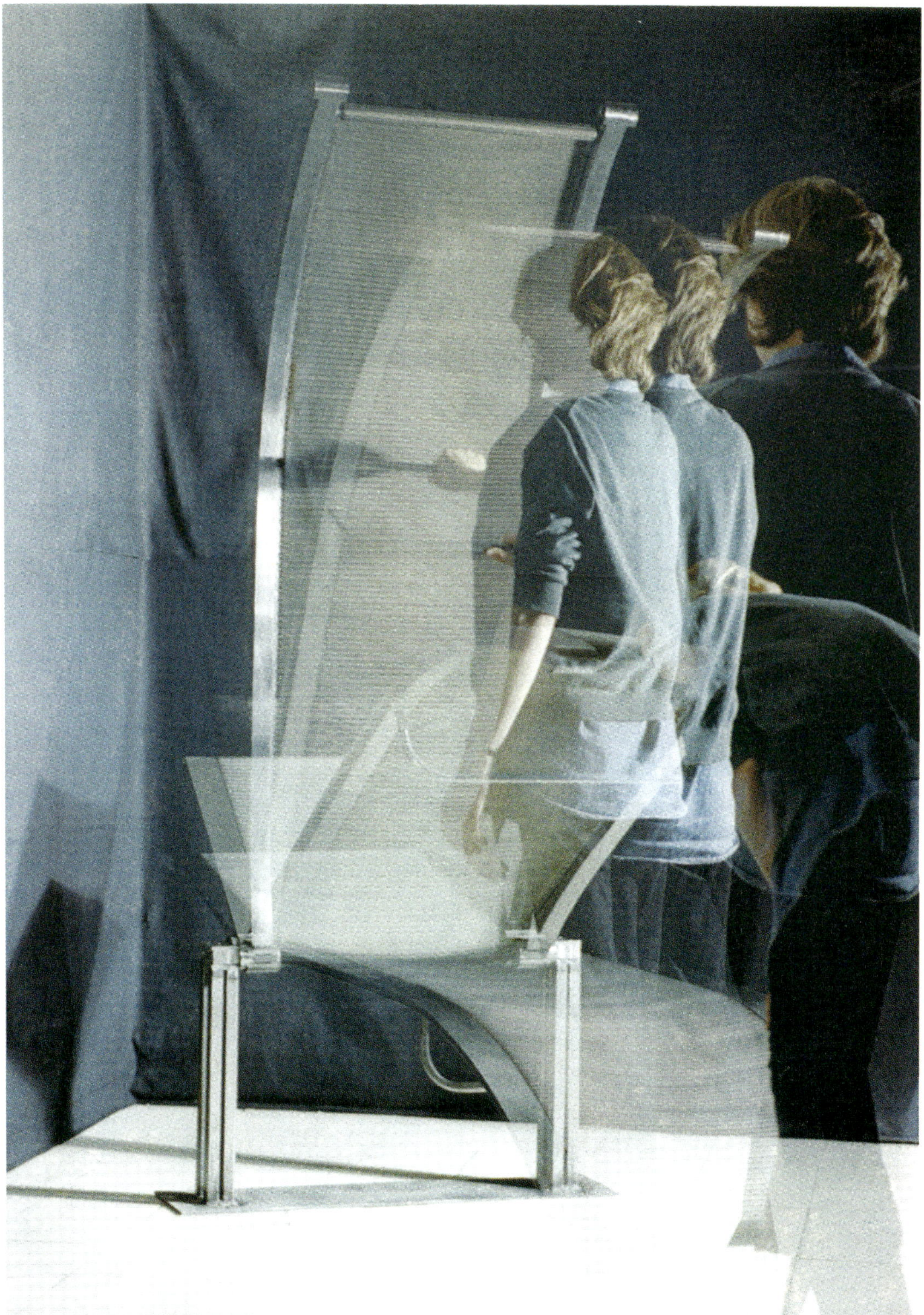

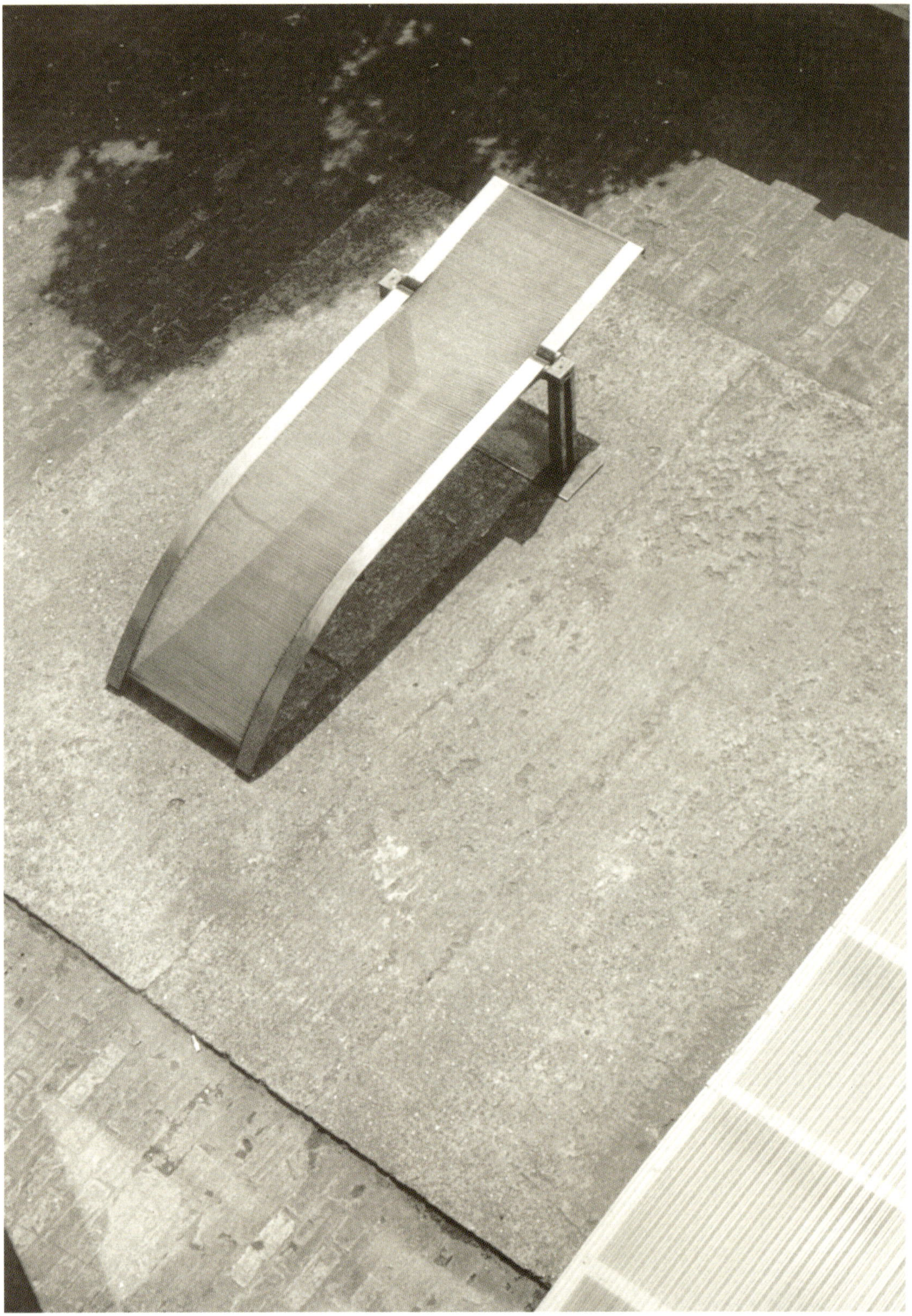

Emma first developed a pivoting mechanism in which the structure 'relaxed' as the bed opened, but the resulting struts confused the form. Her work next turned to the engineering of the joint in combination with a gearing mechanism. These were inspired by the joint of a Rotring compass. The size of the gears initially calculated by the engineering workshop technicians, based on over cautious safety factors, were enormous and clumsy at 150mm diameter and 100mm width. Once engineering calculations were obtained the size of gears halved, and were then reduced still further by the use of high grade steel. After developing a wooden maquette to refine the form of the gears, the gear tooth profile was designed using a CAD program. Each tooth, chosen at a very fine dimension for safety and appearance, has an involute curve which enables it to mesh smoothly and which was undercut to prevent wearing. A test gear set was cut from 5mm aluminium plate and a stop was developed to allow the head section of the bed to cantilever as the lower section rests on the ground.

To control the movement and to hold the bed in the upright position phosphor bronze friction washers were added to the design. The gear is stepped internally to introduce more strength and to provide a bearing surface. As the pin is tightened pressure is exerted by the washers on the gear and the ease of motion is therefore controlled. A locking screw was then inserted to ensure that the pins do not loosen as the bed is opened and closed. A grub screw between the lock screw and pin ensure the two work simultaneously.

The section of the legs attached to the gears was an important development. The width was set by the dimension of the gear at 60mm. Slenderness was the design objective and the legs had to achieve adequate strength over the maximum span of 1.5m. An initial attempt to use a 'T' section only achieved 1/15 of the shear strength required! Emma then turned to a box section which whilst a crude form was, in theory, strong enough. She made lengths in different gauges and found that the lightest gave a slight spring that added to the comfort of the bed even though, theoretically, it was not strong enough. Four methods of making the legs were considered – casting, milling, pressing and welding. The last labour intensive option was adopted because of the machinery and funding available.

Day Bed is inspired by the use of stainless steel link fabric in Ron Arad's highly crafted work of the early 1990s, such as *looploop,* and examples like the simple folding seat in Milan Station itself.

> The metal mesh has many qualities which I like, particularly the *haptic*. In contrast to the smooth cold steel of the legs it is soft to the touch and deforms to the body. It allows the bed to breathe. In the upright position it provides a partial screen, suggesting subtle, but not absolute divisions, still allowing some view in a voyeuristic way. Like the fans used by seventeenth century women to shield and hide, yet allowing the holder to be observant. Tom Dixon challenged me on the question of 'chewing gum and vomit' and, I guess, the mesh can trap dirt, but could easily be blasted with water to clean it.

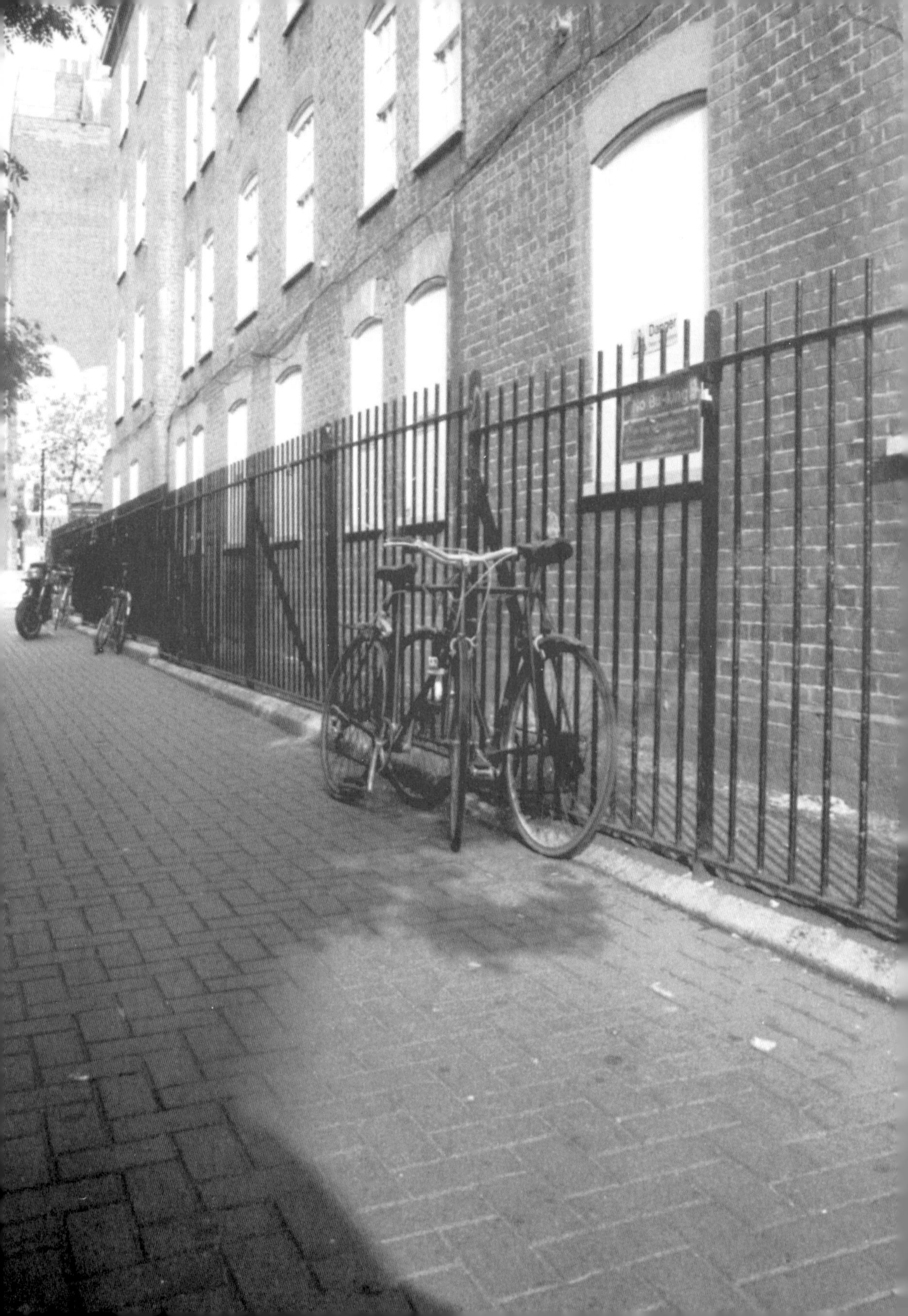

Leaner – José Esteves de Matos

The leaner was a reaction to the cult of privacy and territoriality that is evident in the miles of railing separating the uncomfortable proximity of domesticity and the street in England and London particularly. It was also an attempt to smuggle character into the midst of the symbols of highway control.

The initial intention was to check out the utilitarian mass produced end of street furniture – the plastic replaceable sacrificial buoys, tacky signage and cattle barriers. José's research began with a series of mapped walks in London, followed similar walks in Paris and Oporto. In each city the use of the street was logged and photographed over a diurnal period and a comparative analysis established.

In Oporto the layering and collisions of history coupled with the roller coaster worn topography resulted in the concoction of a series of 'pausing places' at junctions, the widening of streets and left over perimeters.

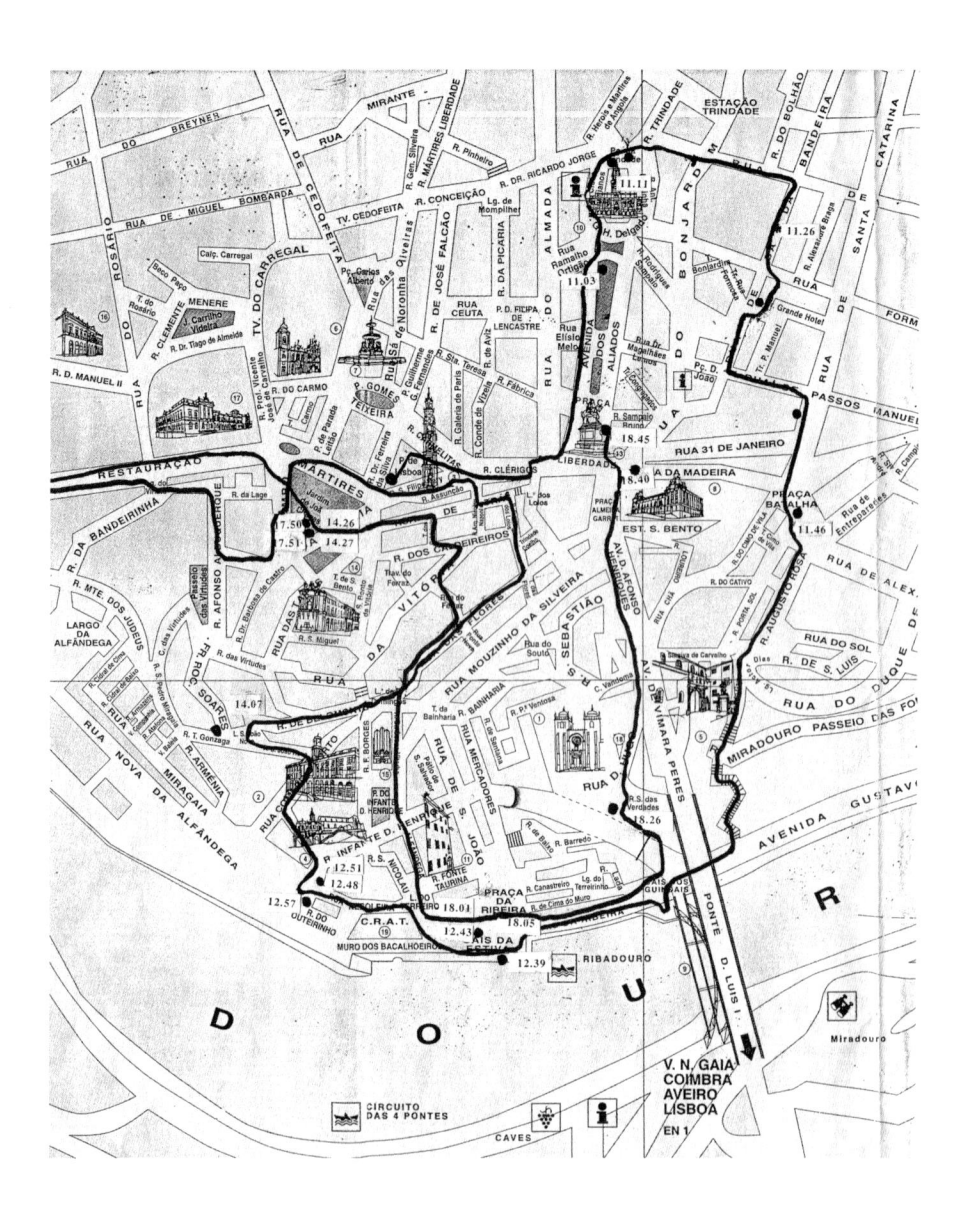

On Certain Possibilities for the Irrational Embellishment of a Town Ten Urban Artefacts

13.36 PLACE ÉMILE GOUDEAU

13.38 PLACE ÉMILE GOUDEAU

18.20 PLACE ÉMILE GOUDEAU

18.24 PLACE ÉMILE GOUDEAU

CAFÉ RIM

DAY 1 LONDON (SUNDAY)

Leaner

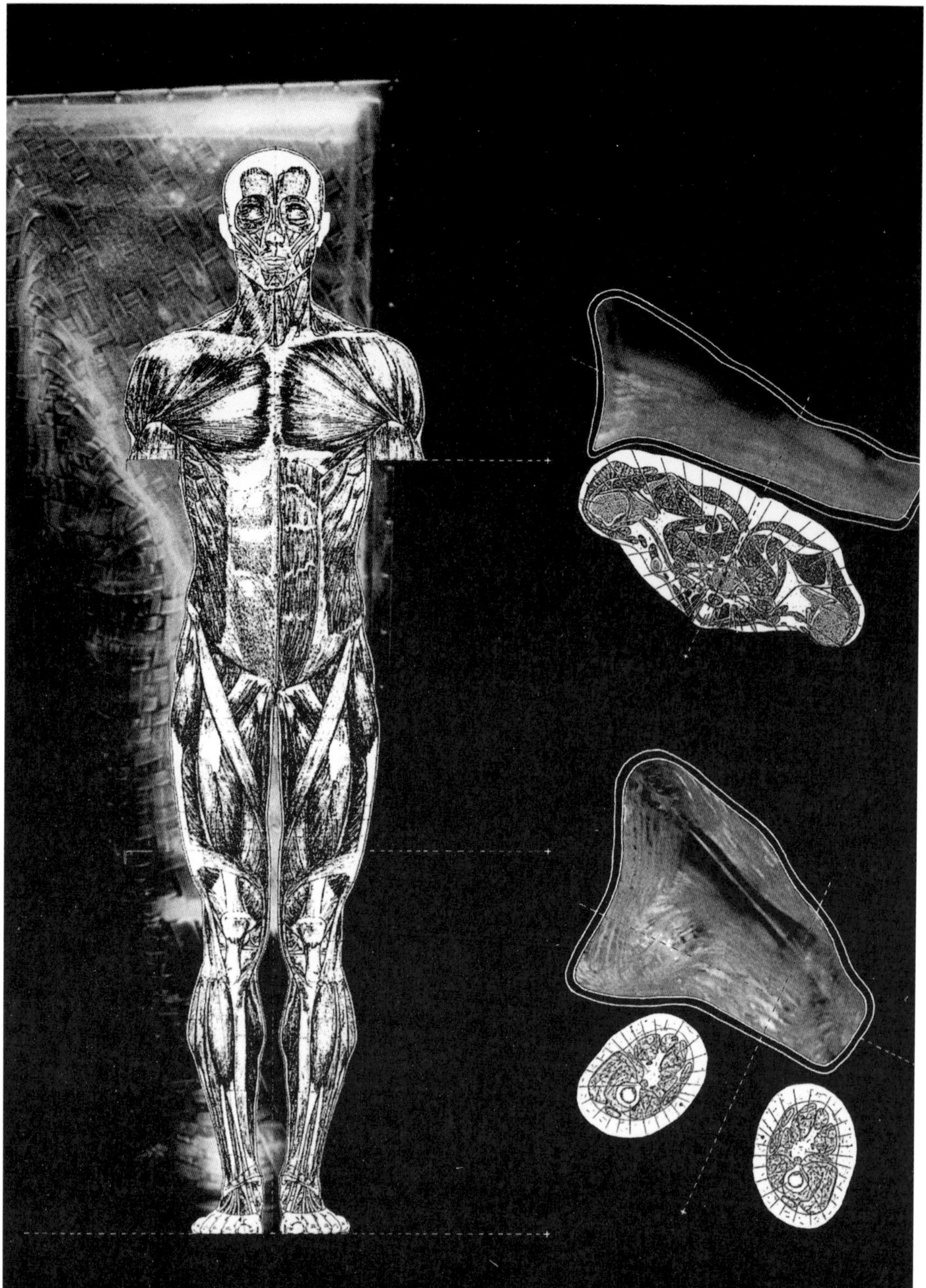

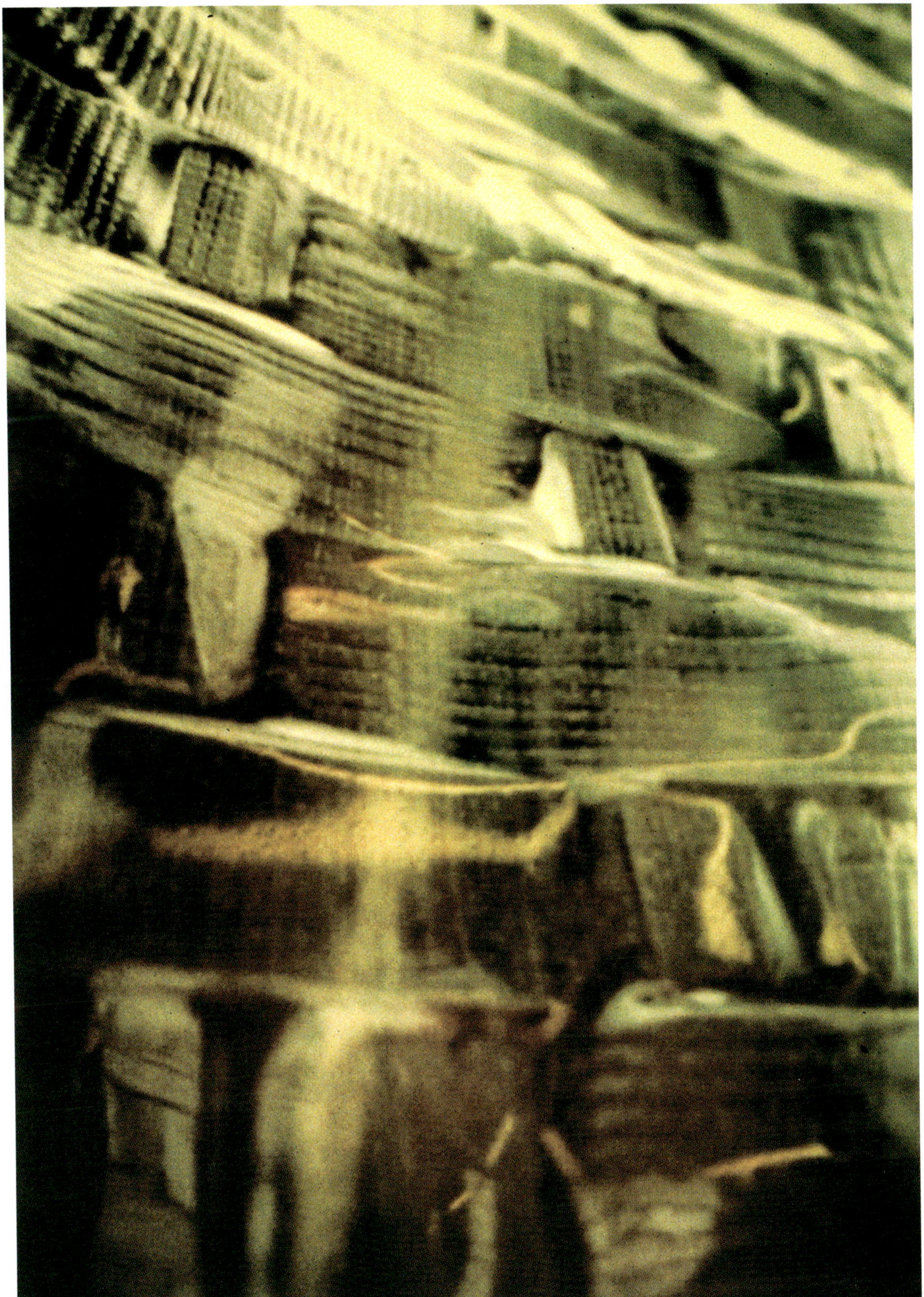

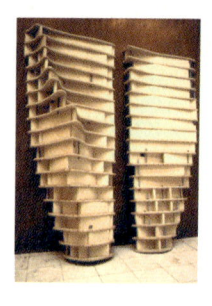

72 On Certain Possibilities for the Irrational Embellishment of a Town Ten Urban Artefacts

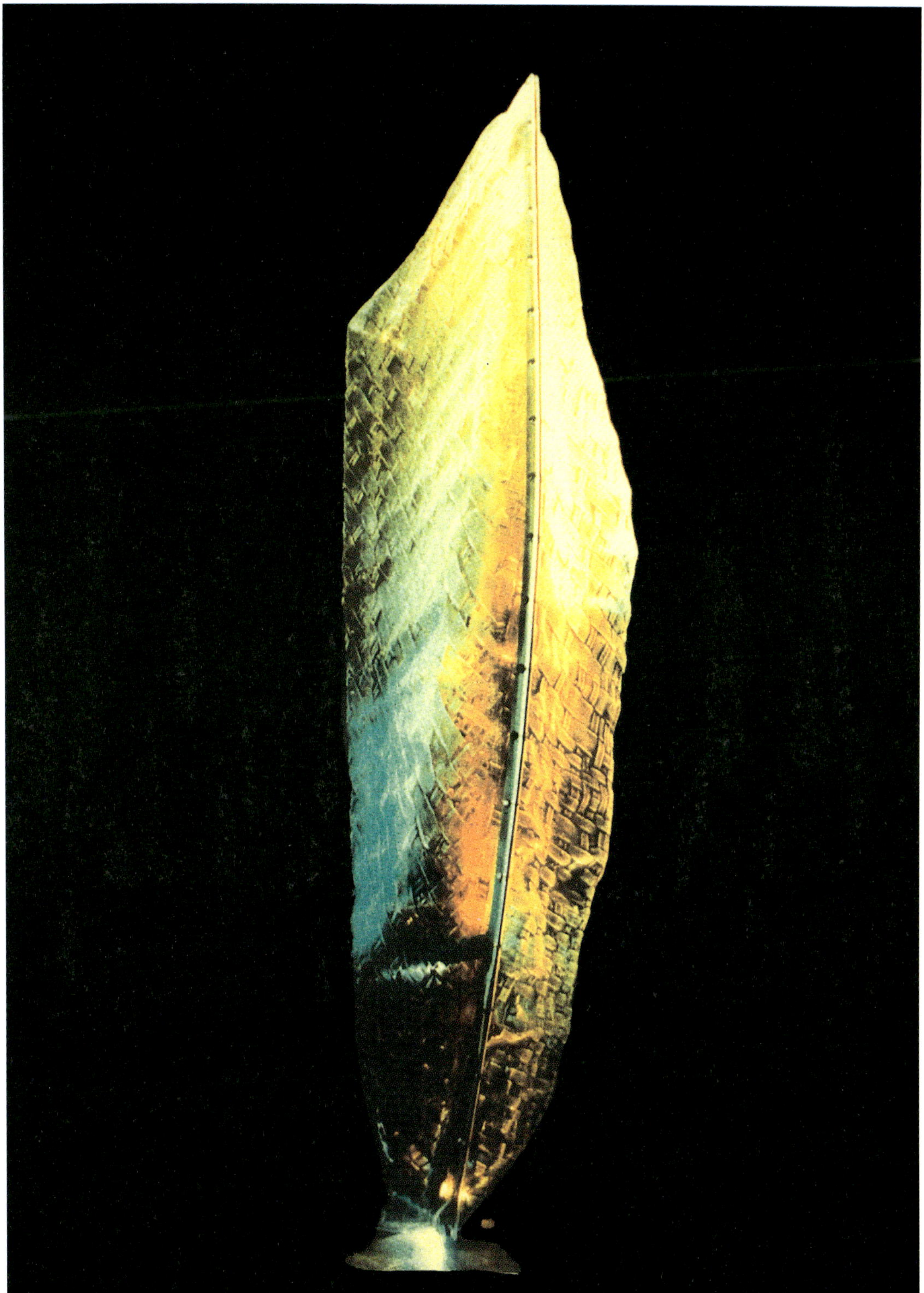

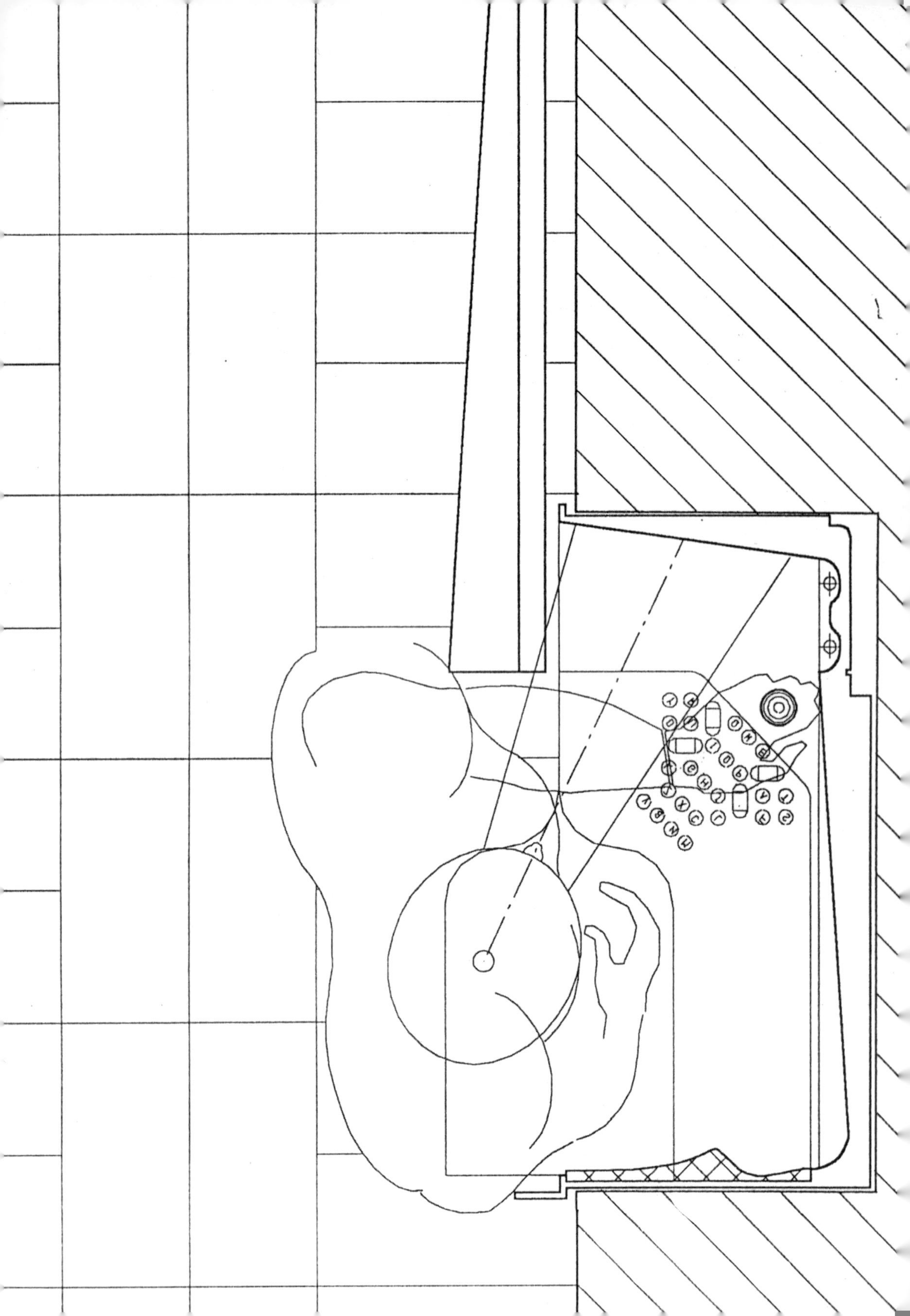

Bitstop – Joseph Marinescu

Joseph Marinescu is a devotee of technology. In 1994 the storm of the internet was still a mild front and he remembers that it was more often than not necessary to explain what the internet was in casual conversations. Part of his mission was to make the internet accessible as a public utility in an object territory between a public phone booth and a cash dispensing machine. His first sketches show a stand alone appliance, a cross between a parking meter and a 1950s salon hair dryer. The size of this 'helmet' was dictated mainly by the size of the then current cathode ray tube technology and liquid crystal display screens, which were small, expensive and provided a crude visual resolution. The idea of an internet booth created the need for a product that did not exist. The first cybercafés were on the horizon, a curious hybrid between the office, post office and café, closer in concept to Andy Warhol's lonely hearts club vision of a diner for single singles, each individual place set with a TV screen, than to a space for conversation in the acoustic privacy of a public room. There was an essential intriguing contradiction between the desire for 24 hour accessibility, needing a public location, and the period of use likely for *Bitstop* which would be an average of 20 minutes – with your back turned to the public world. The second generation of the design was an insectal device, a kind of angle-poise, rather weak, intrusive and ugly – doomed from almost every point of view. The third approach was more promising and offered a number of simultaneous benefits. The idea was to inhabit the thickness of an external wall creating a third plane between the public exterior and the private interior.

This proposal had a number of advantages over the first stumbling attempts. It inhabited and made use of the existing urban fabric. And by creating a kind of wedge it answered some of the issues of vulnerability, as one half of the visual field can be absorbed in the *Bitstop* whilst the other can scan the street. As a niche in a wall there were a number of secondary roles that *Bitstop* could perform, such as being a programmable and interactive advertising screen, missing persons broadsheet or mixed media art project.

The character of *Bitstop* was developed from the interior styling of the Bertone Volvo designed in the mid-1980s, a model of which Joseph owns. Joseph was searching for something of this surprise for the interior of the *Bitstop* – the enticement of a refined and sensual interior camouflaged by a pragmatic shell with a hint of the interior carried through to the exterior. The question of the ergonomics of the interior developed the necessity for a retractable clear skin to protect it.

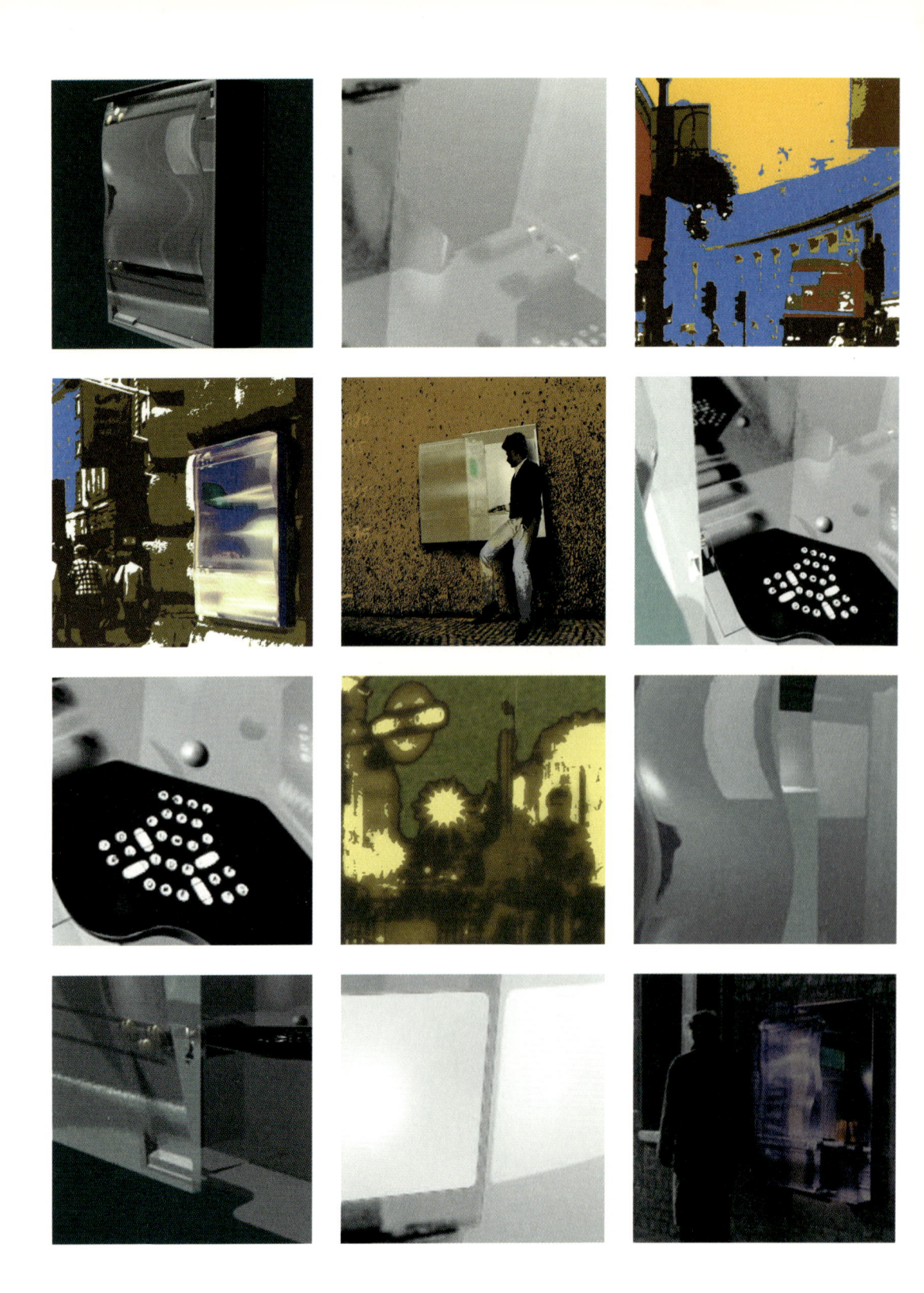

76 **On Certain Possibilities for the Irrational Embellishment of a Town** Ten Urban Artefacts

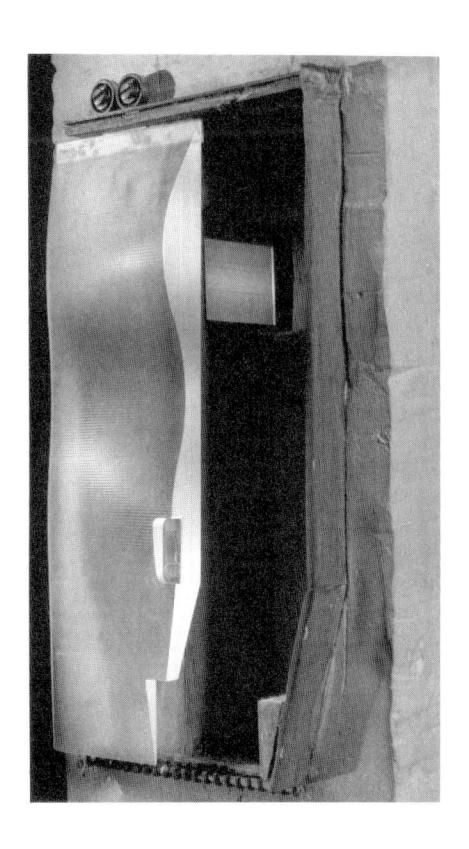

The terminal, embedded in a street wall provides a niche to sit and lean on. The translucent door slides to one side revealing the interior which houses a flat LCD screen oriented towards the viewer with a track ball and key board. Comfort is provided by a retractable bench seat. The housing is made of aluminium, which contains the hardware. The door is milled from polycarbonate and slides on an ingenious set of self-locking stainless steel pins. The seat and arm rest are made of a rubber compound. Both the aluminium body and the polycarbonate door (although acrylic was used for the prototype) were laid out with CAD and the data sent to a computer numeric control milling machine. The initial investigation of the sliding mechanism was directed to sliding door ironmongery, which was generally designed for concealed applications and quite crude in operation. The novel system Joseph designed enables the rolling system to be integrated in the door. The ball bearings were removed from the roller itself and were transferred in pairs to support the shaft of solid rollers which in form are eccentrically mounted on cylinders, allowing for tolerance in each axis.

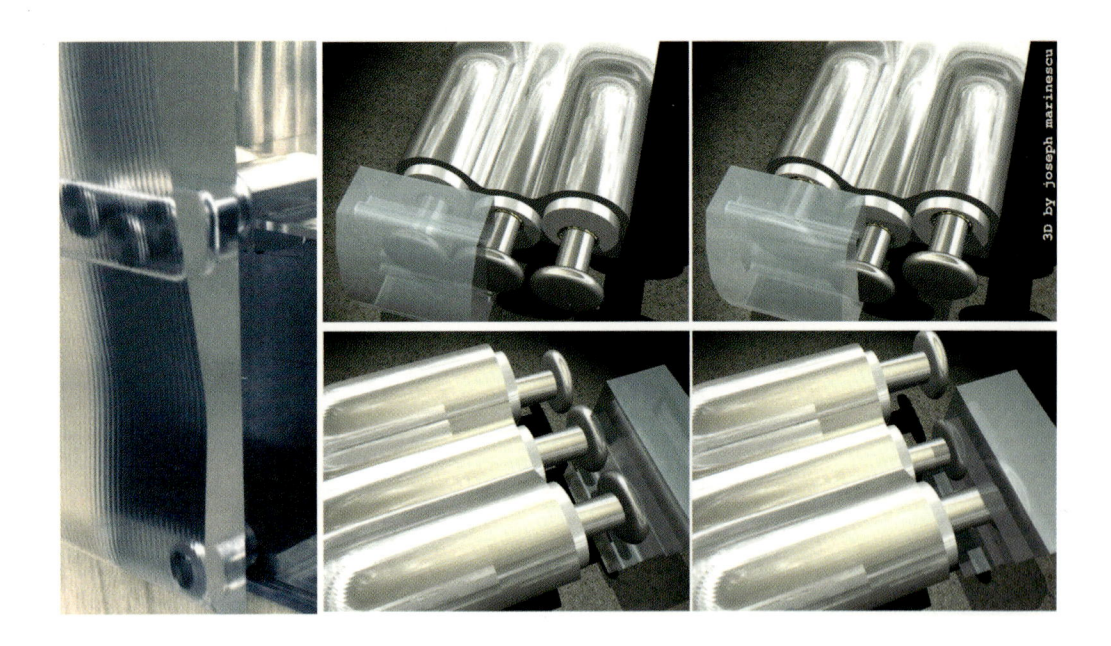

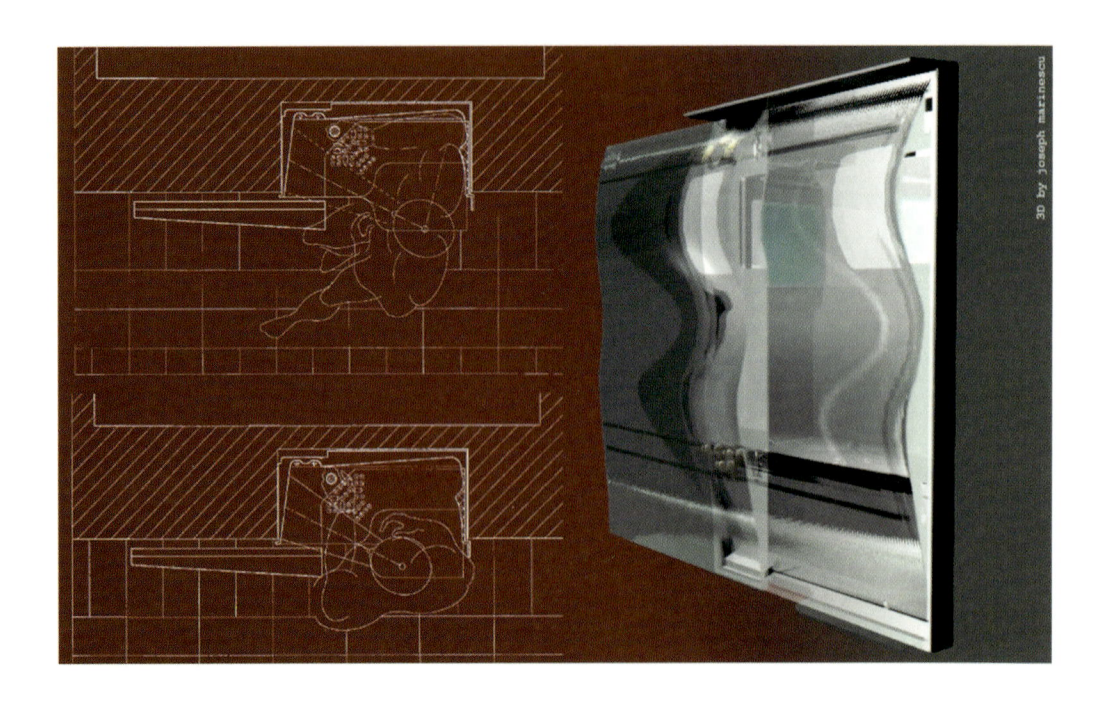

78 **On Certain Possibilities for the Irrational Embellishment of a Town** Ten Urban Artefacts

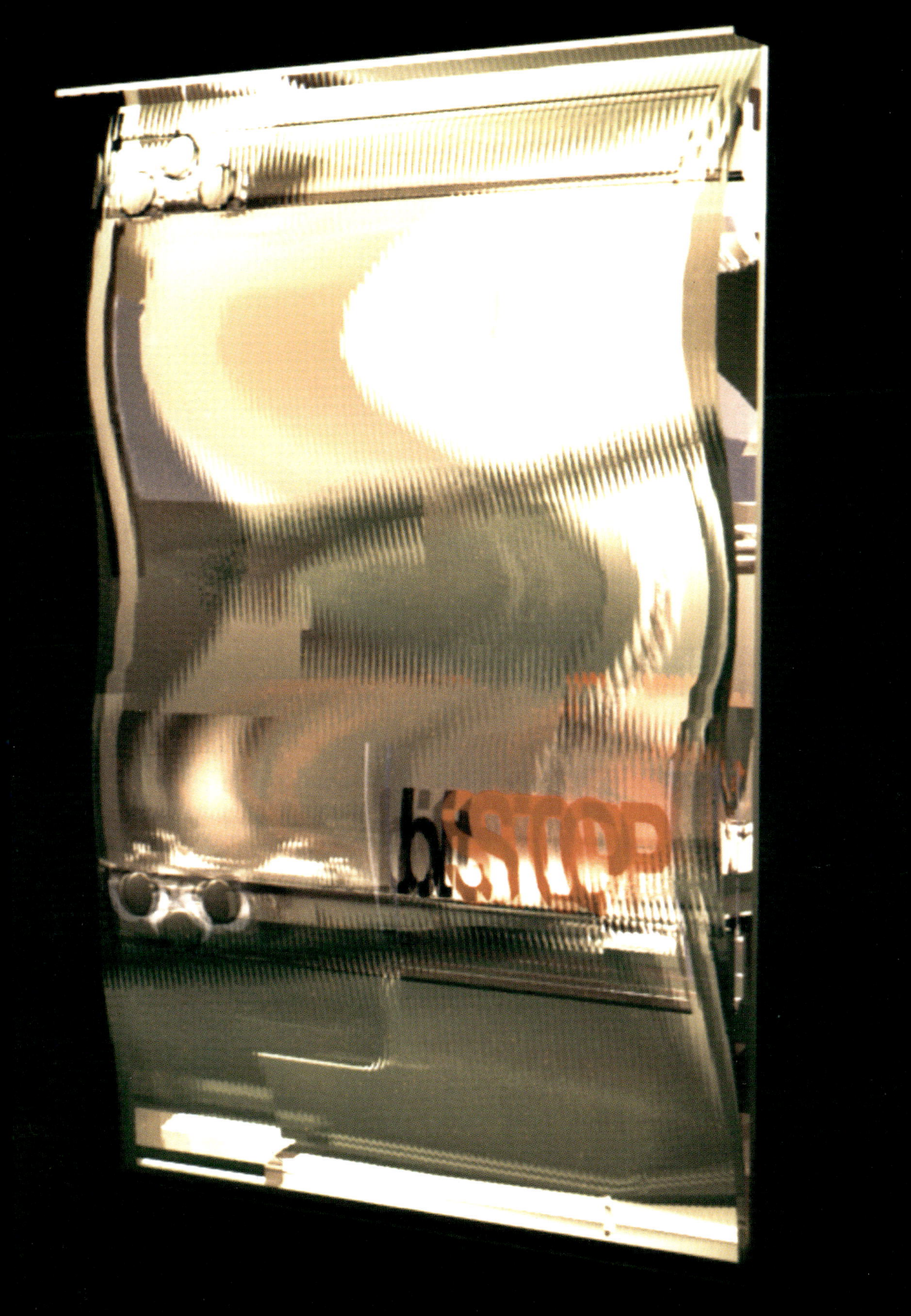
STOP

OBSCURA

Camera Obscura Desk – Anat Taylor

The origins of this table are clearly linked to Anat's early ideas about the psychological tension that exists between the interior and exterior of buildings. It is a central elusive territory for the architect, both an individual signature and yet part of a broader cultural embodiment. It is very much the litmus test of authenticity for a building – the synthesis of issues such as thickness and depth, transparency and opacity, subject and object and the mediation between earth and sky – that envelops the seemingly simple task of drafting a section, plan and elevation. To the town the wall of a building is one part of a greater whole, to the occupier it is the lens through which the world outside is contemplated. This interdependent psychological state is evident in many evocative examples, from the cave paintings of Lascaux to Alexander Pope's grotto at Twickenham, the passage between two worlds in Jean Cocteau's film *Orphee* to Christo's wrapping of the Reichstag.

Anat began her speculations with an investigation of the history of private life, developing her interest in states of being between the private and public – the club, the office – as critical territories in the psychopathology of everyday life. She started to think about walls and the framing of openings that created a view. This led to the dissolution of the wall itself, which becomes an extended frame – a plane on which a picture is hung rather than a spatial boundary. The window dissolves the wall and, eventually, her project was to dissolve the horizontal surface of the desk. Before this point was reached, however, her preoccupations developed into an analysis of the ergonomic relationship between the viewer, the opening, the chair and the desk. Her early designs were trapped by the specifics of the architectural setting – wall and window, floor and ceiling. At this point two parallel precedents began to enfold. The first was the camera obscura, once a painters' friend, an instrument of voyeurism and subject of an intensified reality, but limited by the necessary darkness of the space in which its image dances. The second was the desk. On the one hand this is the ubiquitous industrially designed cell or deep open plan of contemporary office buildings. On the other, it is the specific and personal, as illustrated in Edmund Engelman's haunting images of Freud's apartment just days before his departure from Vienna in 1938. Engleman's description of Freud at works is apposite:

> At first he sat rather stiffly, looking at the camera while I prepared to take his picture, but within a few moments he turned to his desk and became so engrossed in his work that it seemed the outside world had disappeared for him. His writing, in large letters, flowed quickly and without interruption.

The brief developed from the ennui of the sealed box mentality of office letting agents with their jargon of 'flexibility,' 'column free,' 'planning grids,' 'energy efficient,' 'hot desking,' 'clusters,' 'cellular' and the corollary of the air-conditioned deep plan nightmare of office sickness, repetitive strain, isolation, zero personal space, executive chumminess – the reality of much of globalised corporate industry.

WRITING DESK

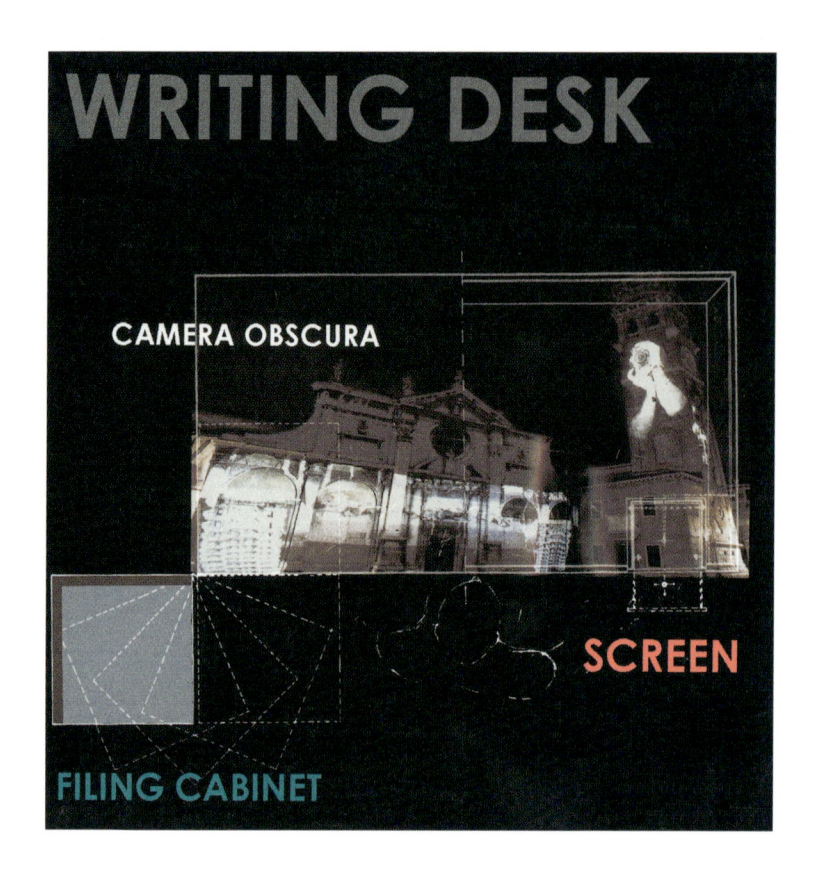

CAMERA OBSCURA

SCREEN

FILING CABINET

82 On Certain Possibilities for the Irrational Embellishment of a Town Ten Urban Artefacts

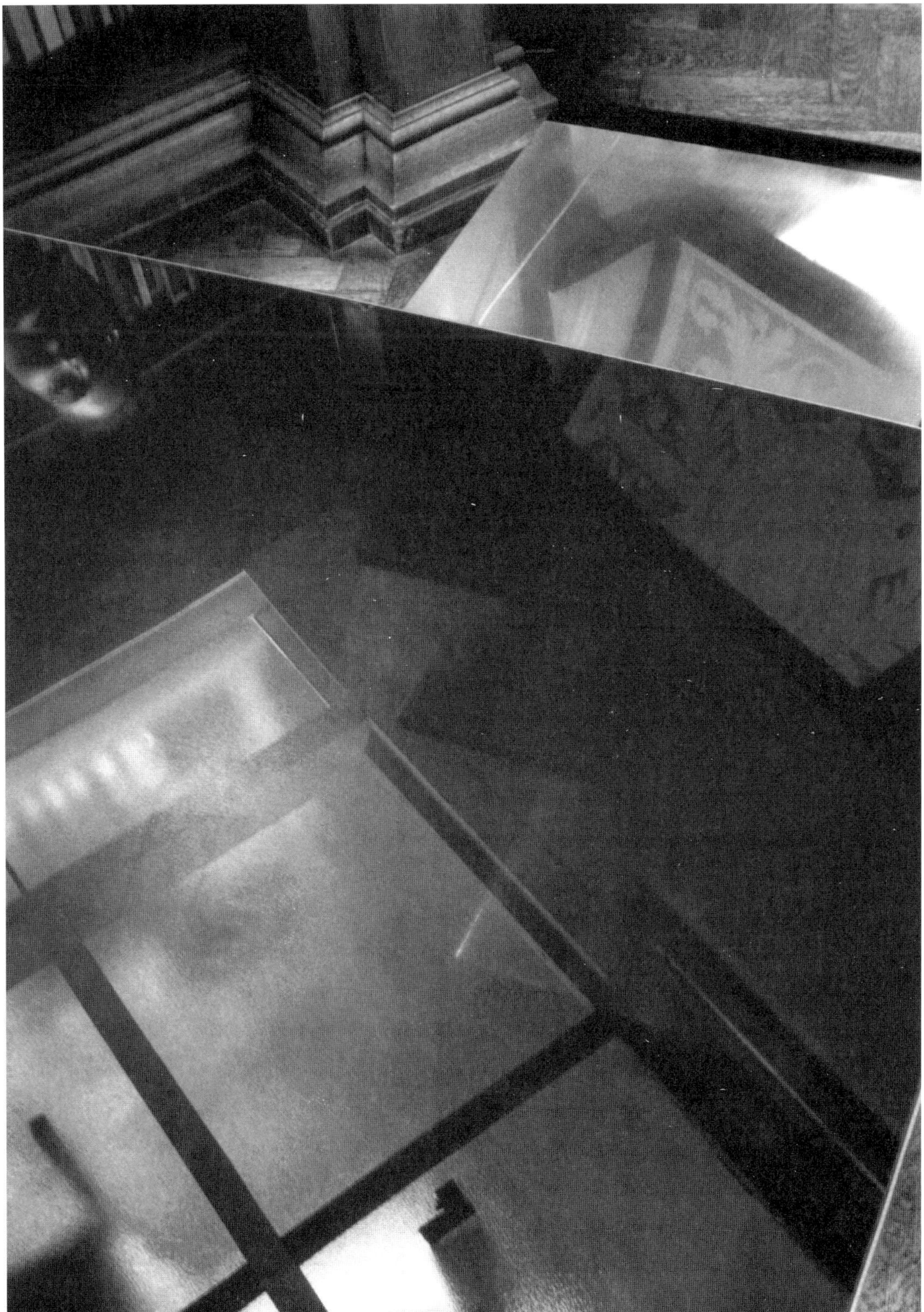

84   **On Certain Possibilities for the Irrational Embellishment of a Town** Ten Urban Artefacts

Camera Obscura Desk

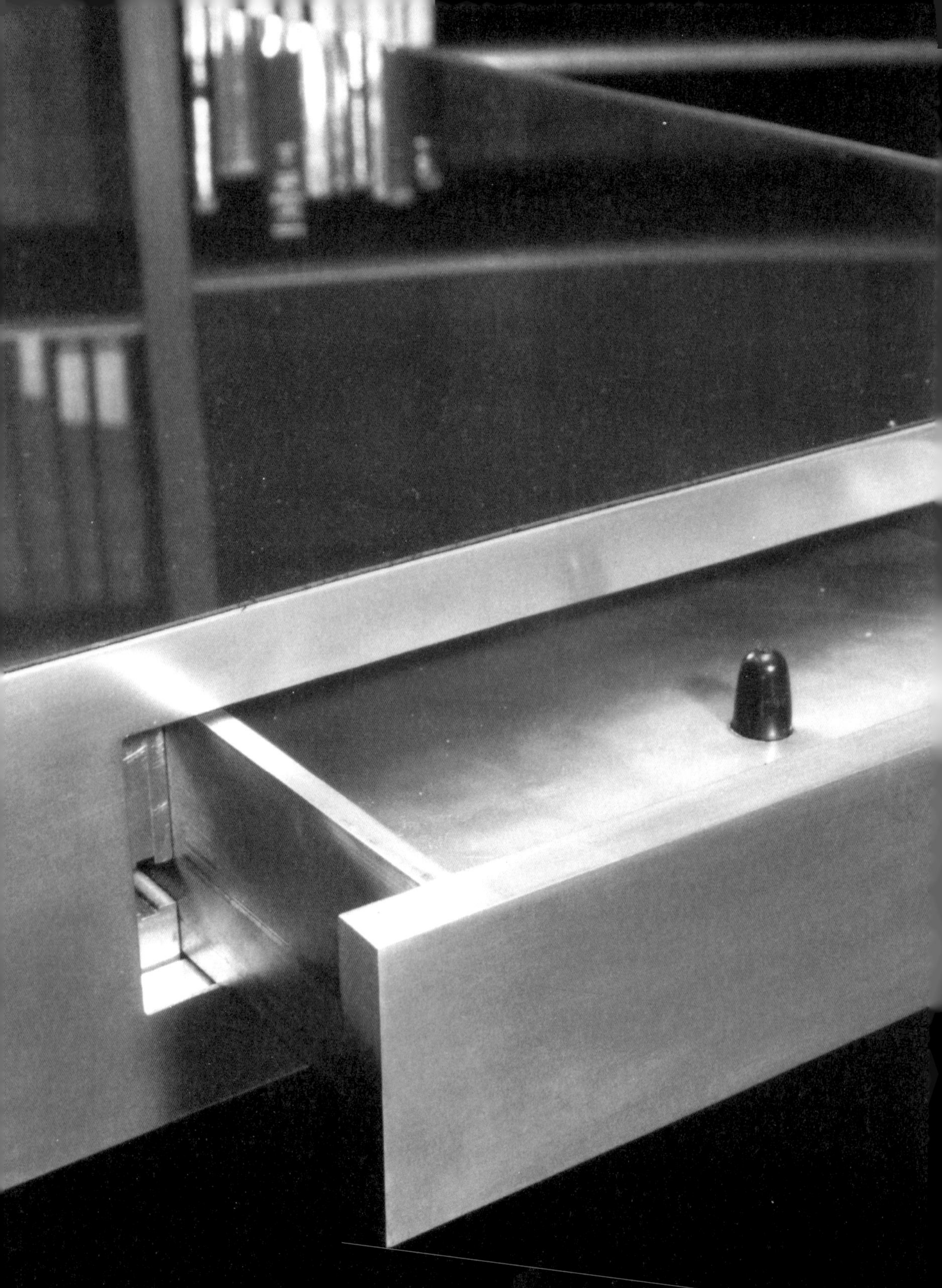

Anat's *Desk* comes alive when, sensing stillness, the smart energy efficient systems turn the zoned lights down. By opening the thin pencil drawer the projector, housed in the raised floor zone below the desk in an outlet the size of a recess power and IT box, is activated. The image is projected to the section of the desktop that, in its closed position, is obscured by a hinged filing cabinet and shelves. The laminated glass surface has an interlayer that enhances the intensity of the image on the glass screen. In the drawer is a finger sized rubber-capped joystick which actuates the orientation of the externally located camera, utilising CCTV technology to achieve the therapeutic connection with a manipulable view of the urban landscape beyond.

In this prototype the dark glass of the desk surface is mounted in an adjustable aluminium frame tapered to maximise the image's location to the edge of the desk surface. As the camera is moved the projected image 'scrolls' across the desk's surface like water to the edge of a weir. The support for this piece is a metal frame to three sides clad in dark lacquered reflective panels. The hardness of the exterior is contrasted with the stretched rubber sheer lining of the interior.

The pragmatic impersonal rendered world of office furniture is profoundly challenged by the witty eroticism of the *Camera Obscura Desk* that turns to advantage so many of the anti-social vices of the works from which it was developed.

Crystal Bench – Erica Cotton

Erica had lived several lives, as an artist, a teacher and a master of aesthetics before turning to architecture. During a part of her long apprenticeship she had surveyed and drawn the external fabric of the crossing tower of Norwich Cathedral and, meditating on the play of daylight on stone, remembered a discussion about how the Cathedral might be lit at night, and the possibilities of the transformation and dematerialisation of structure that lighting offered. The negative corollary was to her the sodium saturation of highways and cities hauntingly illustrated by night satellite images of Europe and their metropolitan hot spots, none more vivid and consumptive than London and the South East of England. London lighting design has belatedly emerged to claim its unrequited potential over the last decade, reflecting new technologies and 90 years of development in the theatre and, latterly, the pyrotechnic lighting of gigs and public festivals. In the theatre Adolphe Appia and, particularly, Gordon Craig developed the idea of transformation through light with movable panels and screens – lit at the front to create an illusion of interior and from behind that of an exterior. Erica, always critical and hesitant, began to collect a powerful set of precedents, the accuracy of her intention is clear when with hindsight you see the echoes of these first thoughts in her finished work: the spire of All Souls Langham Place, lit from its base, the bare fluted conical geometry levitating from the parapet and body of the church below to leave it floating like a spectre above Regent Street; the follies of Bernard Tschumi's Parc de La Villette, colour by day candescent by night – work intriguingly between the scale of furniture and building. Ideas began to converge – the light initially without scale, an object that could have been a skyscraper or a table lamp vertical or maybe leaning, and the bench a meeting place, a place of gathering, both physically and mentally, a stopping place, a horizontal floating plane. And then, closely following, the idea of counter-balance, scaleless like one of Iakov Tchernikhov's formal exercises cocerning planar intersections. Erica worked with models alone, tentatively introducing materials that would develop into the precisely tuned and differentiated elements of the *Crystal Bench*.

As the maquettes progressed there is a reassurance in the development of their apparent instability, the light leaning like the crystal of a geological fault. The bench floats, a wing of metal supported on a twisted stem that is seemingly too insubstantial to be stable. During the day, light is captured in the crystal creating a glow against the backdrop of the more absorbent greens of the parkscape and the greys and browns of the street, whilst at night the crystal becomes a light source.

On Certain Possibilities for the Irrational Embellishment of a Town Ten Urban Artefacts

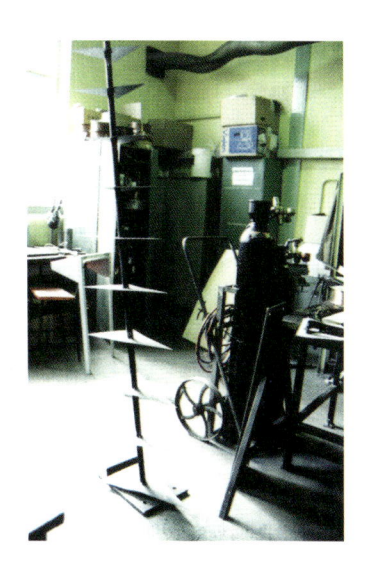

Crystal Bench

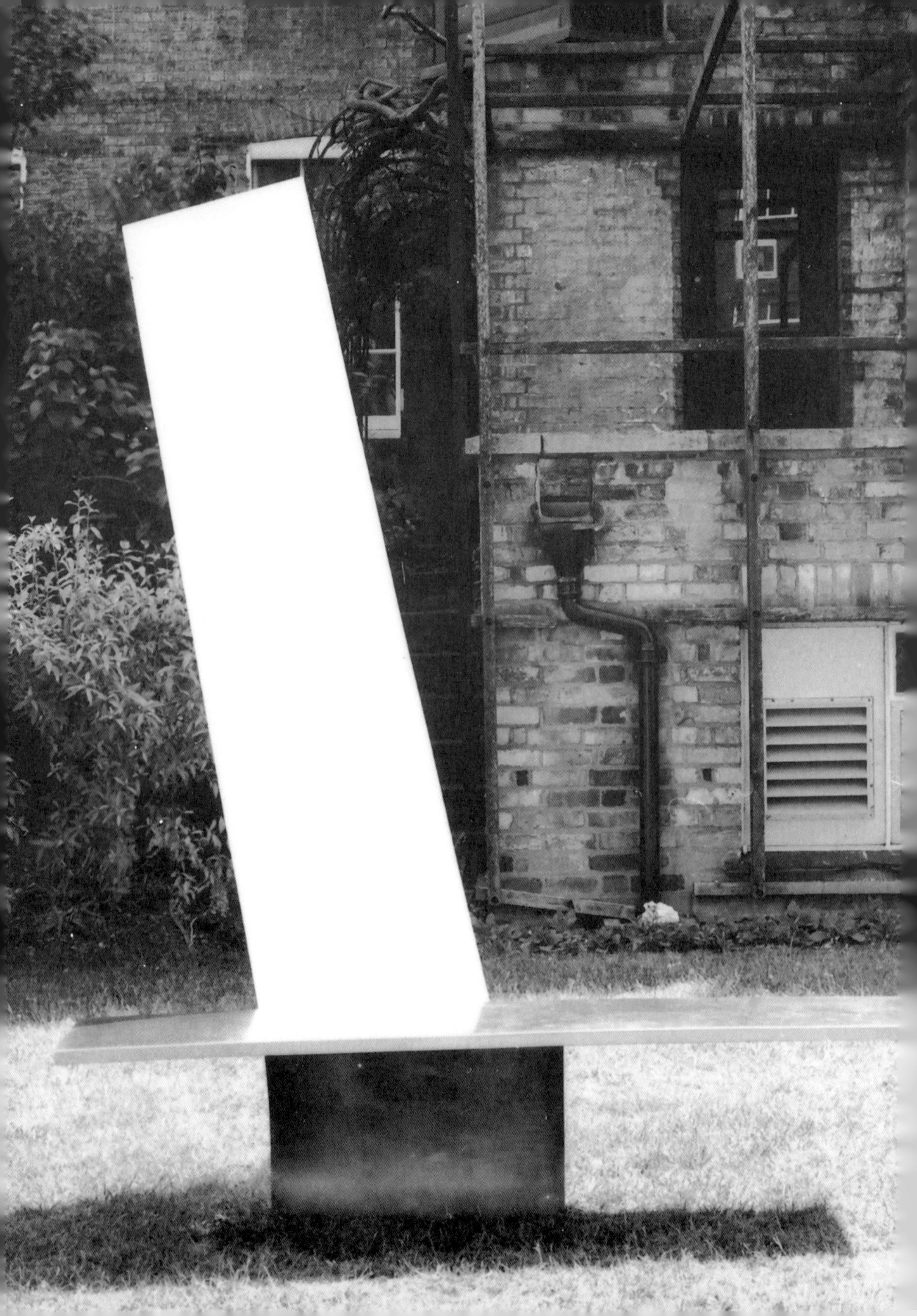

Erica's working method was closer to sculpture than architecture, moving from a pocket sized maquette to half scale models, with mock-ups at full scale being made before moving to the works' final material translation. The form of the crystal evolved with the intention that the final piece was to be made from perspex sheet.

The subtle implications of the chosen form meant that, rather than extracting the triangular plan from a fixed base to a resultant diminished triangle at the tip through three straight lines, the triangles at the top and the bottom were twisted creating a set of curved spiralling edges and planes. The twist of one leading edge was made with solid sections of timber onto which hardboard planes were fixed. Once this was completed, a measured survey was made at 250mm vertical intervals. These were translated into a series of metal triangular plates that were welded, with some consequent deviation, to a central metal spine set to the intended angle to form a jig for the construction of the perspex case. The crystal was limited in size by the economic availability of perspex sheet. The edges of the sheets were hand mitred to create a continuous 1.5mm gap and a bonding agent was syringed into the void to create a single welded crystal.

Acknowledgements

Particular thanks to my co-tutors Signy Svalastoga and Robert Kennett.

And also: Peter Carl, Phil Cooper, Steve Denton, Tom Dixon, David Green, Chester Jones, Samuel Lesley, Nick Rhodes, Albert Taylor and Richard Christmas and all the technicians of the Department of Engineering workshop at the University of Cambridge.

Thanks to Edward Woodman for his photographs of *Borderline*.

The publication of *On Certain Possibilities* has been, in part, financially supported by the University of Cambridge Department of Architecture

These urban artefacts began as a series of seminars and ended with an exhibition at the Department of Architecture, University of Cambridge in June 1996. They were carried out as the work of ten individuals in a Diploma Unit taught by Eric Parry.

Colofon

On Certain Possibilities for the Irrational
Embellishment of a Town

© 2000 Black Dog Publishing Limited and the authors.
All rights reserved.

All opinions expressed in material contained within
this publication are those of the authors and not
necessarily those of the publisher.

No part of this publication may be reproduced, stored
in a retrieval system, or transmitted, in any form or
by any means, electronic, mechanical, photocopying,
recording, or otherwise, without the prior permission
of the publisher.

Produced by Duncan McCorquodale.
Designed by Mono.

Printed in the European Union.

ISBN 1-901033-77-5

British Library cataloguing-in-publication data.
A catalogue record for this book is available from
The British Library.

Black Dog Publishing Limited
PO Box 3082
London NW1 UK
T: 020 76922697
F: 020 76922698
e: info@bdp.demon.co.uk